Morocco to Timbuktu: An Arabian Adventure

The book of the BBC2 series

By Alice Morrison

This book is dedicated to the Team: Harry Bell, Alicia Arce, Séamas McCracken, Laura Buchan, Charlie Shepherd, Ben and Ismaiel Dicko

Edited by: Tanya Woolf   tanya@tanyawoolf.co.uk

Chapter List

Thanks

Chapter One

"The distance and the hardship of the road they travel are great. They have to cross the difficult desert that is made almost inaccessible by fear and beset by the danger of thirst. Water is found there only in a few well-known spots to which caravan guides lead the way. The distance of this road is braved only by a very few."

Ibn Khaldun, Al Muqaddima, 1374 -8

Squinting through his one good eye, Abd El Raheem passed me the long, silver hashish pipe. The rest of the boat crew looked on with keen interest. Adventuring credentials on the line, I inhaled with fake relish, trying to look as though smoking dope at 9 am on a fishing boat bound for Tangier with a band of reprobates, who would have put Johnny Depp to shame, was my normal Friday.

It was day one of the shoot for "From Here to Timbuktu" a two part series for BBC 2 where we were trying to unearth the old trade routes which had flourished for hundreds of years from the heart of Europe, right through Morocco and down across the Sahara to Timbuktu.

Caravans of gold, ostrich feathers and slaves had come north. Caravans of salt, tools, cloth and leather had gone south. Precious books and manuscripts spread the vast stores of scientific, political and literary riches that the Islamic lands gathered as Europe stagnated in the Dark Ages.

It was going to prove quite the adventure, but on day one I was more worried about whether I could do the job, than crossing the Sahara.

It was my first time presenting for TV and the Executive Producer for Tern TV, Harry Bell, had already put the fear of God into me.

"Have you any idea how rare it is," he said, fixing me with a gimlet stare, "for a presenter with absolutely no experience whatsoever to get to do a series. It is unheard of. Completely - unheard - of."

No pressure then.

Any TV programme is the sum of all the people who work on it, and we were going to have to be a tight crew to get through it and make that magic happen. We were a motley bunch. Dinner the night before had been our first chance to get to know each other and as the red wine flowed, the anecdotes came fast and furious.

James Cutting, one of our Moroccan fixers, a bon viveur with a Leslie Phillips laugh, made a strong start.

"I was in a bar in Zimbabwe," he said, "At the Falls. Behind the barman was a glass case with a severed human arm in it. It belonged to a man who had been bitten by a black mamba while out in the bush. When the mamba bites, you have only 30 minutes to live. It acts like frostbite but is fatal. Knowing this, he took out his machete and chopped his own arm off. He never bought another drink..."

Alicia, our Director and so the boss, countered strongly with graphic pictures of her leg. Bloody, swollen and full of pus, it made me decide against creme caramel for desert. She had picked up an infection in Africa which had started eating through her flesh.

All heads now swivelled to Toby, James' partner in crime. His father had been a body double for James Bond. In the sixties, he and his beautiful, blonde bride had driven over to Marrakech in a Bentley. James now lives on a farm outside Marrakech.

"'One night on the farm," he said, "we heard noises of shovels clanking and digging. When we got up in the morning, there was a big hole in the ground that looked like it had been left by a chest. What we think had happened is that treasure hunters had come through and using an old map had found something. There is lots of treasure buried hereabouts - especially silver. But the treasure hunters believe that silver is cursed with evil spirits - jinn - so to cleanse it, they have children dig it up, and then they sacrifice them so the blood will purify the metal."

Feeling I ought to contribute something, I mentally flicked through my store. Pigmies and steaming elephant liver? Nasty bedfellows in a Syrian brothel? A hundred hornet stings? Hmmm. None of them quite cut the mustard. Just as I was rallying myself, Séamas McCracken, our cameraman and a lover of poetry and mountain biking came in with the killer and I knew I had nothing to come back with.

"I was filming on a hovercraft in the Belfast Lough on a very cold and windy November day, when the hovercraft decided not to hover anymore. Not only did it cease to hover – it started to sink and there I was in the freezing water. I had the newest and latest BBC camera with me. My protective clothing was a thick woolly jumper that felt like a dead body hanging on to me. I did have a life jacket on and so I managed to hold the camera up above the water. The rescue boat arrived, took the camera and promptly disappeared for the safety of the shore. About thirty minutes later another boat braved the conditions and came and fished us out of the water. I was so cold I couldn't move my arms anymore. I couldn't really speak either, but that was because I'd put my brand, new watch in my mouth to keep it out of the water. I think I probably had hypothermia because I then slept for 10 hours straight. Later, I got a call from the BBC – they were calling to check on the condition of the camera."

Back to our boat.

We had hired a local fishing boat to get us into Tangier to start our journey at the nearest crossing point to Europe. Only about eight miles separate Europe and Africa there and the channel is swimmable on a good day. Tangier was the main port of trade between the two and is a city that has been fought over by everyone from the Romans and Phoenicians to the Portuguese, Spanish, French and British.

It's also where the great Arab conquest of Spain started from, although the initial invading force was made up primarily of Berbers. In 711, the great General Tariq Ibn Ziyyad, left Tangier, crossed the straits and landed at Gibraltar which took his name – Jebel means hill in Arabic so Tariq's Hill, Jebel Tariq, morphed into Gibraltar. From there, he swept across Spain and laid the foundations of the Cordova Caliphate. The story is that when he was crossing the straits, the Spanish didn't take much notice as they thought the ships were just traders, so they were caught unawares.

Our boat wasn't a trader, it was a stubby trawler which fished the waters of the channel and was painted in the bright blue and white that is typical in Morocco. I had expected to be clambering over nets when we got in but was told by the captain that net fishing was outlawed and that they only fished with lines. That seemed like hard work to make a living to me. He had a crew of four and the costs of the boat and the fuel to pay for as well as port dues, but he said that in fact they did quite well as they would get up to £20 a kilo for the "Bardyo" fish and these weighed up to 80 kilos.

The captain was a dead ringer for Captain Haddock, but slightly more grizzled. He was called Abd el Wahid (the Slave of The One) and had a bushy beard, proper sailor's cap and an explosion of wrinkles when he laughed. We bonded immediately. He told me that he had been at sea for 39 years and had sailed all over the world, including doing some spells on Russian ships. He had a wife and nine kids back in port and seemed to be a man very happy with his life. It wasn't long before I was allowed to take the helm, and I even got to borrow the cap.

It couldn't have been a more perfect day with bright sun and a clear sky, very little wind and flat calm. That was until the ferries passed us and then we were bobbing around in their wake. Laura, the Assistant Producer, started to feel a bit queasy and gulped down some seasickness tablets.

"No, no," said Abd el Wahid when he saw her and scooped up a bottle of sea water. "You have to drink from the sea so you can balance your stomach with the outside." He took a healthy gulp, to demonstrate. I swallowed a mouthful or two to show willing, and Laura lay down in the bow with her hat over her eyes, groaning gently.

My smugness at feeling chipper was about to be shattered. We were nearly at the port and it was time for my first piece to camera. How hard can it be, I thought? Well, I soon found out.

With a piece to camera, the way it works is that you decide roughly what points you want to cover and how long it should be with the director. Then the cameraman plonks you in the place where he can get the best shot and makes sure your face has got some light on it. In this case, it was right on the prow of the boat, as near as I could get to the sea. It wasn't too rough but I kept my hand on the railings just in case, as I didn't fancy a shot of me upending in the water to become a star turn on the Christmas bloopers show. The director and assistant producer stand out of camera range with the assistant producer listening for meaning and mistakes and the director, head down over the monitor, watching the shot. Behind them, was the fixer and a very interested crew, ready to watch the fun.

It was extremely intimidating and I felt like a plonker.

Take one.

"Action," says Alicia, and I am off, out of the traps, babbling. I am definitely trying too hard. The expressions on the row of faces in front of me range from uncomprehending but pleasantly amused (the crew) to decidedly anxious (Alicia).

Take two:

"You look like you are thinking too hard. "

Take three:

"Keep the energy up."

Take four:

"Less enthusiasm."

Take five:

"Can you be more enthusiastic but not so smiley."

Take six:

"Can you be a bit more spontaneous."

We keep working at it and eventually Alicia unlocks it for me by telling me to be a bit more chatty and I relax down. Bingo. Having spent a large part of my TV-viewing time looking enviously at the Ben Fogles of this world and thinking, "Ha, I could do that, he has got the cushiest job in the world," it was a rude awakening.

From the port in Tangier, you can walk across the road, through one of the ancient gates and straight into the old walled city, the medina. It is all based on a hill, so you are either walking steeply up or steeply down, through winding alleys past little shops. Right beside the main gate, there is a huge mural of one of Tangier's most famous sons, and my historical crush, the famous Arab historian, Ibn Battuta.

I studied Arabic at university and one of the books I attempted was "The Journey" by Ibn Battuta. I sweated blood over that text, having to look up every third word and often coming up with complete jibberish as a translation, but it fired my imagination.

Born in 1304, he was to become one of the greatest travellers of all time, journeying around the world three times as far as Marco Polo. Samarkand, Constantinople, Sumatra, Chittagong, Dharfour – the places he visited are a litany of bucket-list travel, and most importantly from my point of view, he got to Timbuktu in 1352 and wrote one of the first accounts of the capital of what was then a great empire.

He had travelled across the Sahara by caravan along the old trade routes which is exactly what we wanted to do. Strange to think of me ploughing through those texts all those years ago and now having the opportunity to actually follow in his footsteps. Fate? Whatever it was, I was taking it.

Timbuktu. Everybody knows the name but it is one of those places that you are not sure actually exists and, if it does, where it is. A good pub quiz question. In 2006, a survey of 150 young Brits found that 34% did not believe the city existed at all, and the other 66% thought it was "a mythical place". In Collin's Dictionary, it is still defined as meaning "any outlandish or distant place." So,I was approaching this quest for Timbuktu a bit like a treasure hunt, hoping that along the route we would find clues and traces from the great trading past.

Whenever I imagined Timbuktu, I had in mind an El Dorado, a shining city of gold in the desert. This was in large part due to the story of Timbuktu's greatest King Mansa Musa. Mansa Musa was the richest man in history – well, so says Time magazine - and from Timbuktu he ruled an empire which extended over 2000 miles. Crucially, in this empire, he had the gold mines of west Africa, which provided much of the gold that eventually ended up as European coinage. One of his many titles was Lord of the Mines of Wangara.

In 1324, as a good Muslim, he embarked on his pilgrimage to Mecca, and by all accounts it was a fantastic affair. He set off with 60,000 men of whom 12,000 were slaves who carried four pounds of gold bars each. He was preceded by heralds all dressed in silk, brandishing gold staffs. There were also a reported 80 "gold" camels who carried up to 300 pounds of gold dust each.

He also took his own household of wives and children. En route, one of his wives complained to him that she missed bathing in the waters of the Niger. She was clearly a favourite because he stopped the entourage and set some of his 60,000 men to work. They were tasked with diverting the course of the river to create a natural lake for her, which they did, so she could bathe in peace and be reminded of home.

The most amazing tale from the journey, though, concerns gold. As a Muslim, you are obligated to give out 10% of your earnings or wealth as alms or zakat. In Mansa Musa's case, he did this in gold and very liberally. In fact, he distributed so much gold to the poor of Cairo, that he crashed the economy and inflation went sky high. It took ten years for the economy to recover, but I am willing to bet that he left a lot of poor people very happy.

The fame of his wealth spread throughout Europe and in 1375 it was immortalized in one of the earliest extant maps of the region, the Atlas Catalan. The map was commissioned for Charles VI of France and can still be seen in the National Library of France. It was researched and created by Abraham Creques, a Jewish cartographer from Palma and it covers the known world at that time from the Canary Islands to China. Drawn on the panels, which cover the empire of Ghana including Timbuktu, are two little illustrations. One of my historical crush, Ibn Battuta, looking a bit uncomfortable on his camel, and the other of Mansa Musa with a crown and sceptre clutching a whacking big nugget of gold.

"Alicia," I asked, "When can I talk about Mansa Musa and his extraordinarily large nugget?"

She looked at me sternly, "Alice, this is not just about you waltzing across Africa making fna fna innuendoes…."

We were heading towards the gold market to see whether we could find any remnants from the Timbuktu gold trade. If you've ever been to the gold suqs in one of the Middle Eastern countries like Dubai or Saudi or Oman, you will be visualizing dazzling displays of jewels in dozens of shop windows. Millions of pounds worth of stuff crammed into one area and crowds of black robed women handing over wedges of cash. Adjust your expectations for the Tangier gold suq, it is a much more modest affair.

It is situated at the top of the hill along one main, winding alley. We had arranged to meet our Tangier fixer at the bottom to be guided up. His name was Saaid, a huge man with terrible teeth and a magnificent Norfolk jacket. An amiable chap, he had only one fault.He was allergic to any kind of effort.

We set off up the hill towards the suq. Laura, our assistant producer, mistress of the one liners, and with a fabulous Out of Africa wardrobe, was gamely struggling upwards carrying the tripod which was very heavy. Saaid must have weighed four of her.

"Saaid, my friend," I asked winningly, "Could you help Laura and carry the tripod?" I fully expected the normal Moroccan response which is, "Of course, no problem". But no.

"I would love to," he said, "If only I could. But I have The Sciatica." The capital letters were there in his voice.

Gold fever. It is something you hear about but I have never really understood it. To me, gold is just a nice, shiny metal which looks pretty on earrings but that is about it. This trip has changed that and it started with my meeting Maha Alouani a cultural anthropologist, an expert in Moroccan trade routes and also passionate about the music of Mali. She is currently the manager of the Heritage Museum in Marrakech which she set up with her parents.

She was there to tell me all about the gold that had come up from Mali, through Morocco and ended up in Europe. The gold originated in the mines of West Africa, was brought across the Sahara and minted in Morocco, often by Jewish coiners. From there it would make its way through Tangier and into Spain and then spread through to the rest of Europe. We were about to see our first physical clue from Timbuktu.

Crammed together in a tiny shop, Maha and I and the shop owner peered at the little coin in her hand. It was only about the size of a one pence piece but it exercised an attraction that far outweighed its size. Once I had got it in my hand, I felt an overwhelming desire to keep it.

Knowing it was a physical part of the history of the routes we were exploring was a part of it but, even more than that, was the sheer, sparkling prettiness of the thing. It looked valuable in the way that a pile of notes just can't replicate. I could feel its story. It had been dug up somewhere in West Africa by miners labouring under the hot sun. It had then been transported thousands of miles across the Sahara by camels, and been traded up to just outside Marrakech where it had been minted and stored by some merchant as part of his solid capital or exchanged for goods.

Round the rim of the coin were Arabic inscriptions which I couldn't quite make out but Maha explained.

"It says that it was stamped in Aghmat on the way to Ourika not far from Marrakech and it says that it is Abdulawiya ,which meant it is from the Merenid dynasty of the 15th century. Gold was exchanged in the north primarily for salt and slaves. It was used to print coins for trade but also to adorn palace walls and even for day-to-day transactions."

The greatest Moroccan Ruler of that time was called Ahmad El Mansour Al Dhahabi – Al Dhahabi means golden and he was given the nickname because of his love of the stuff. He had enormous territorial ambitions and sacked Timbuktu at one point. His lasting legacy is the Badi Palace in Marrakech which, when it was built, was the wonder of its age. In 1594 an English merchant noted a caravan coming up from Timbuktu with around 3,000 kilos of gold and it has also been written that there were 1,400 men working on hammering out gold ornamentation at any one time at the palace gates.

When this coin was in circulation, it could have been used for something as banal as the weekly shop in the market but now the coins are highly prized by collectors. The gold itself is very pure at 21 carats but, of course, it is the history that makes them so desirable. Wealthy individuals buy them up and create small museums and collections in their homes in Morocco. Sadly, I was not to join their number and had to give up my treasure to Maha to keep safe. I really did feel a Gollum-like pang as I handed it over.

Tangier's history is not just about trade. Its strategic geography, international mix of residents, easy access to the Rif mountains and large quantities of narcotics, and laid back vibe also made it a gathering place for spies during and after the World Wars and then the Beat poets of the sixties.

Glamour, intrigue and sleazy encounters centred around the Petit Socco, a square in the medina. I was not in search of cheap sex or drugs, but was desperately in need of a strong, black coffee as we parked ourselves at one of the open air cafes to regroup and have a look at the map. I was just taking my first sip when I heard a familiar voice.

"Alice! Bonjour, ca va? Qu'est -ce que tu fais ici?"

It was my upstairs neighbour from Marrakech, Jean Louis, who also owns a Masion D'Hotes in Tangier. I immediately felt like a local, very gratifying. The aim though was to have a look at our map and think about where the rest of the adventure was going to take us.

Now, I like to think I have done quite a bit of travelling, and quite a bit of adventuring in remote places, but the sad fact of the matter is that I find equating maps to reality virtually impossible and I have no sense of direction whatsoever. I can get lost just stepping outside of my flat. When people give me instructions that start with, "Go east on highway 2...." they may as well be speaking Japanese, a language that I am entirely unfamiliar with. I am sure that my friends think I am just being lazy and that if I made more effort I would be able to map read and navigate with the best of them, but I honestly think it is a kind of word/image/directional blindness. I find my way by landmarks. It is the only way I can do it.

It was with some trepidation, therefore, that I rolled out the map that the Tern TV graphics team had made up based on the old manuscripts that charted the main trading routes across the Sahara. How pleased was I when I discovered it was my kind of map. Pointy things to show mountains, wavy dunes for the desert, palm trees and camels scattered appropriately and gold triangles for the gold mines. The main centres of the trade routes were marked: Tangier, Fez, Marrakech, Sijilmasa, Guelmim and Timbuktu. The routes themselves were clearly marked out across the whole of North Africa right across to Cairo, crossing different parts of the Sahara but all converging on Timbuktu.

As you would expect with a trading history that extended over numerous empires and several centuries, there are a lot of route options to choose from. These had changed, emerged or disappeared as the centuries wore on and political and economic realities changed.

In the 1500s, the merchants faced great dangers crossing the Sahara. Many of them were natural ones. Running out of water or food, getting lost, facing sandstorms all played their part. Of course, banditry was another danger for the traders and was one of the reasons they liked to travel in large caravans.

Those natural dangers remain, but now it is political and people-caused problems which make vast areas impassable. Political tensions mean that the Moroccan-Algerian border is a closed one. The unresolved dispute of the Western Sahara ensures that large areas to the south of Morocco are closed to us too. Finally, the rise of extremism and the presence of Al Qaeda and related groups, as well as Touareg separatists, make the Sahara a dangerous place to roam in. Add to that the smuggling gangs that bring everything from cigarettes and drugs to people looking for a new life in Europe across the desert and you have a pretty explosive mix.

Our ambition was to follow the main north-south salt and gold trade route as closely as possible. In Zagora in the south of Morocco, there is a sign saying 52 days to Timbuktu. The map makes it looks so easy, but it is absolutely clear that it won't be and I know we are going to have to be very creative to get to our goal – Timbuktu. That is for another day though, with the Atlas mountains and the Chebbi Dunes to cross first, and for now I was happy to trace the route on the map and think of the infinite possibilities ahead.

Most of my big adventures up to this point have been physical ones: the Tour D'Afrique, cycling from Cairo to Cape Town; the Marathon des Sables, running six marathons across the desert back to back carrying all your own food and equipment; the Atlas to Atlantic trek, hiking from the highest point in North Africa at 4167 metres, straight across the Atlas mountains to the sea. From Here to Timbuktu was different as it was more of an exploration and a discovery. To that end, I wanted to get about the country using as many different local methods of transport as possible. There'll be more about how I defied death on a donkey cart later but from Tangier to our next stop of Fez, I'd decided to hop into one of the Grand Taxis – the shared local taxis.

These all go from outside the central station. Grand taxis are traditionally either yellow or white ancient battered Mercedes which can accommodate six passengers and a driver. In an effort to modernize and also to improve safety, the Moroccan government is phasing them out which feels rather sad, but for now if you want to get somewhere cheaply, and don't mind a squeeze then you're going to find yourself in a Mercedes.

The taxi square was full of its usual noise and bustle when we arrived. Big tourist buses with their mirrors that look like the horns of a bull, people selling nuts and dates for the trip, and a poor lad, off his head on glue, begging for some change. There was also someone selling long strings of bark that smelled of licorice. It was the first time I had seen them and it turned out they were a natural toothbrush and flossing system all in one.

The taxi drivers were parked up in rows, shouting out their destination. "Chaouen, Chaouen, Chaouen." No good to me. "Marrakech, Marrakech, Marrakech." Nope. Then finally, "Fez, Fez, Fez." I had found my ride. Abdul, the driver, was a big bear of man with a rather superior white Mercedes which had the luxury of springs in the back seat. We set off with just two of us as passengers; myself and Driss. Abdul was confident that we would pick up more passengers as we got to Qunaytra. Not adverse to a back seat that normally fits four, for just me and Driss, I settled back for a chat.

Driss was a very dapper gentleman. Slim and white haired in an impeccable jellaba and neat skull cap, I felt rather disheveled beside him even though I had both brushed my hair and put on lipstick that morning. He was travelling to Fez to buy some merchandise. A modern-day trader. For over thirty years, he told me, he had been doing the same thing. Buying souvenirs in Fez - teapots, jewellery and other things that tourists might like - for 100 to 150 dirhams and then selling them on in the medina in Tangier for a profit of between 50 and 100 dirhams. He didn't have a shop but had always just worked from the street and made a good enough living to bring up and educate four children. He spoke seven languages, including English, and talked to me in all of them. We stopped for lunch at a popular roadside restaurant where the animal carcasses are hanging up opposite the cooking area. You choose which cut you want and then the chef cooks them over the grill and adds chips and salad. We met up with the crew who were following us and managed to eat a staggering three kilos of meat between the nine of us. The chips were greeted with wild joy. Hungry work, filming.

Back in the car, I couldn't keep my eyes open and indulged in a power nap as did Driss. After Qunaytra, we started to pick up passengers as Abdul had predicted and our spacious back seat was soon full. These trips are always very jolly as you get to meet all sorts of random people. I had had the forethought to bring some cashews, and once I whipped those out, we were definitely the party car. Cashews break down all cultural barriers. Conversation ranged across the full spectrum, from Scottish independence to the crops growing in the fields along the way but the road took up a lot of attention. The government is building a big new highway with excellent drainage, as the road we were on often gets flooded when the rains come which blocks traffic between Tangier and all the towns on the way to Fez. There was some very satisfying tutting and moaning about how long the works were taking. Clearly this is a universal human trait. But there was also agreement that it was a good initiative and would benefit everyone in the area so, on the whole, a happy bunch of citizens.

Our taxi mates hopped out along the route and new ones came in, keeping the trip lively. The sun got lower and lower and I was glad that we were all squashed in the back as it started to get really cold. We arrived in Fez as the sun disappeared and bade each other a fond farewell. It had taken me just a few hours to travel the distance that it would have taken the traders a couple of days to cover. The adventure had started.

Chapter Two

"Travelling – it leaves you speechless, then turns you into a storyteller."

Ibn Battuta

As Charlie Shepherd always says, 'Fez is for connoisseurs." He's right. Fez has always been the intellectual and Islamic centre of Morocco and has one of the oldest and largest medinas in the world. It used to be rivalled by Aleppo but, tragically, Aleppo's old suq has now been largely destroyed. Like Rome, Fez is set on hills, with the warren of the old walled city in a small valley, and there is a magic about it.

Charlie had joined us the night before. He was to be our main fixer for the Morocco leg of the trip. We had run the Marathon des Sables (MdS) together. Well, when I say together, what I mean is that we set off for each stage together and we were tentmates. He was much, much faster than me. MdS is called the toughest footrace on earth and it is a 156 mile ultra race across the desert. You basically do six marathons in six days, and, to make it harder, the middle one is a double. Also, you have to carry all your own food and equipment for the race yourself. It was Charlie who had made me totally anal about how much my back pack would weigh to the extent that I cut the handle off my toothpaste to save 9 grams.

He'd been running an adventure company in Morocco for 13 years and knew everything and everywhere in the country.

Walk through the streets in the early morning through any town in Morocco and you will be assaulted by the smell of fresh bread. I wanted to get an idea of what the merchants would have eaten on their journey and, of course, bread was a staple. It has always been baked in communal ovens and I was going to one to meet Najat Kaanache who is an expert on the history of Moroccan food. Najat is a rather extraordinary woman. A Berber, her family had moved to Spain to find a better life and, from that background, she has risen to become one of the world's great chefs. She has cooked in many Michelin starred restaurants, has her own cooking programme and owns restaurants all over the world, including a new one in Fez. She's a wild, gypsy of a woman with masses of black hair and always wears layers of brilliantly-coloured skirts and scarves, pinned together with flowers and spangles. Being with her is like being swept up by a glittering tornado.

The bread shop was a hobbit-like, warm paradise. My nostrils were flared out like an indignant horse to take in the smell of the bread, cakes and thyme-topped biscuits. The baker stands in a pit in front of what is essentially an enormous pizza oven. He has big wooden paddles which he slides the bread in and out of the oven with. He makes some of the bread himself to sell to customers, also shop and stall holders but a large part of his work is to bake the bread that the local women bring in. Traditionally, you may well not have an oven in your house, so you bring your dough down in the morning and pick up your loaves when they are ready. This means, of course, that the baker knows everything that is going on in the neighbourhood. Gossip and carbs in one fell swoop.

Next stop on the food tour was the meat and vegetable market. This is a feast for the senses. Fat, sweet bananas and mandarins lined up beside rows of fresh mint. Baskets of dried red chillies next to baskets of live snails. Snail soup is very popular in Morocco, so I guess these little fellows were just awaiting a watery grave. I don't mind the soup but have to say that the snails don't look that delicious crawling around a basket. Our aim was the camel meat stalls, as camel meat and milk would have been eaten and drunk on the route. You can tell which is the camel meat stall because it very handily has a severed camel's head dangling outside. I tried not to look at the dewy eyes, with their long eyelashes. The meat itself looks like best beef. It is red and not at all fatty. All the fat is in the hump. The hump was there separately, like a little pyramid of white and the butcher shaved off bits of it so that we could use it when we were cooking.

For foreigners there can be a bit of a taboo about eating camel meat, explained Najat.

"It's good meat, people underestimate this, it's amazing. People think that you are cruel when you eat a camel. People have that magical emotion or attachment to the camel because it's something touristic… it's like an attraction, a camel. If you're seeing a camel, you're like "oh it's a camel!". But we have to explain that for centuries this has been a way of eating also. It is part of our culture and we still have to preserve it. Even if we have internet, and we have TV and everything, people still eat the way they used to eat. So we have to respect that."

I decided that if there was any good time to start eating camel, it was when it was to be cooked by a Michelin-starred chef. Armed with our bag of prime camel fillet and our little poche of hump, we headed back to Nur where I was going to be allowed to cook with Najaat.

As soon as we got into the kitchen, my delightful shopping companion transformed into a Generalissimo and I was the squaddie. After five minutes I knew that I would never be able to survive Masterchef. Camel meatballs were on the menu and we rolled the meat and a little bit of fat together with some fresh local herbs and spices. I was soon shooed out, as Najat went on to prepare lunch for the whole crew.

I am sure that when the merchants reached Fez from Timbuktu, they feasted, but I am willing to bet they didn't feast like we did that day. Charles, Najaat's partner, had laid out a long table in the middle of the riad, which was all tiled in black and white, with sunlight flooding down through the roof. He then went outside to invite Mohammed our cart pusher in to join us for lunch. You can't drive in the medina and we had a lot of heavy camera kit, so we had hired Mohammed and his cart to help us. I loved Charles for that. The meal was amazing: camel meatballs, beetroot and blanched radish salad with grapefruit, smoked salmon on saffron bread….. I tucked in but looked up to see Laura, not eating and with a worried look on her face.

"It's time. We're behind schedule. With every mouthful, I'm casting sequences away in my mind," she said.

That night, I was to sleep in a caravanserai, a foundouk. These are the old staging posts for merchants which are to be found all over the old towns and cities of North Africa and the Middle East. It is where you would come to stable your animals, store your goods and spend the night. Now, they are often converted into little shops or used as workshops for ceramicists, wood workers, leather workers and ironmongers.

I walked down from the main gate of Bou Jouloud behind a man who had two white, live chickens hanging over his shoulder. My foundouk was on the left going down the hill. I arrived just as the sun was setting, so the little shops inside were mainly closed.

You got into the foundouk through an enormous wooden arched door that looked as though it had been there for centuries. Once inside there was an open courtyard with the shops around it. A leather one had its goods at the front and in the back a group of workers were busily stitching away at bags and pouffes. When this was used as a staging post, the animals would have been stabled in the shops and in some of them you can still see the tethering rings – lower down for mules, higher up for camels. In the bigger, back rooms, there was plenty of room for animal feed and the merchants' goods.

Upstairs were the human quarters and a spare room was waiting for me. Initially, I was slightly anxious because I had been warned that the caravanserai are used now by the homeless to sleep in, and there is a problem with glue sniffing and also (perhaps surprisingly) alcoholism. Also, it is considered very odd for a woman to stay alone in this kind of building. But this foundouk had its huge doors to shut against the world and a guardian, a woman, Fatima, so I felt pretty confident as the doors clanged to, almost squashing a black kitten that squeezed through at the last minute, also looking for a place to sleep.

The upper storey, mirrored the bottom one, with rooms arranged around a square roof over the courtyard beneath. This area was covered in drying animal hides and washing. There were about eight rooms up there and each one housed a family. The single toilet and sink were downstairs beside the shops. As I went up to sort out my stuff, I could hear all the evening sounds that you would expect: cooking, the TV, kids playing, and someone who clearly had smoked way too many cigarettes coughing their lungs out.

Morocco is cold in the winter and none of the buildings are designed for warmth so I had brought all my kit with me. A good sleeping bag, a sleeping mat, my blow-up pillow with the fleecy cover, a head torch, a little solid fuel stove with some rooibos teabags, sugar and some sweet cakes from the bakery. Most importantly of all, I had my warm, pink, fluffy, 100 percent acrylic pyjamas with little white love hearts on them.

I had to do a video diary that night and Alicia had warned me.

"Alice, you are absolutely NOT allowed to wear those fluffy pyjamas if you do a video diary. On. No. Account."

"But, Alicia. I bet Bear Grylls would wear these if he could. They are so warm."

"No."

I was unpacking everything and settling down when my first visitors arrived. Two little girls aged around eight and six. They came in and we got chatting as they turned everything over and helped me make my bed and blow my pillow up. Minutes later, their Mum, Malika arrived with her little baby boy, Abdel Hadi, and the guardian, Fatima. It was shaping up into a sleepover. Thank goodness I had bought the cakes. I fired up the little stove to make some tea and started offering around the cakes. Malika hurried off to bring glasses, mint, dates and a little chair to sit on. Fatima took one look at my sleeping arrangements and left to come back with two extra blankets one for under and one for over.

Both Malika and Fatima had lived in the foundouk all their lives. Malika told me she had recently moved to have a bigger room where she and her husband and three children slept, cooked, ate and lived together. I asked them what they cooked on and they told me a gas ring powered by a butagas cylinder. Anything that needed to be baked could be taken to the baker's oven. Both the girls were at school and both could speak some words of French which made their mother very proud. I taught them some English which they picked up immediately with the usual Moroccan flair for languages.

They were very curious about me and predictably horrified when I said I wasn't married and didn't have children. It is so alien a concept in this society that even though I am very happy with my life choices, I always feel like a weirdo when I try to explain why. My feeble attempts to persuade them of the joys of freedom and an independent life were brushed aside and we got down to the much more interesting job of listing the qualities that were needed in a husband and then contemplating their list of single male relatives and friends who might be suitable. We all agreed that sincerity, kindness, and a stable income were necessary. I said I wanted my husband to have teeth and Malika reassured me on one point.

"Don't worry about your age," she said. "You are still beautiful even though you are so old. And you know, the prophet Mohammed married Khadija and she was fifteen years older than him!"

Party over. I slept like a log but woke early. I steeled myself for the toilet downstairs and opened the door. I nearly died of shock. There was Alicia with a camera, standing totally silent in the dark. She had crept over early from the hotel and hadn't wanted to knock in case I was doing a video diary.

We set off for the top of the hill where the Merenid tombs lie to watch the sunrise. The call to prayer started and then was taken up note by note all over the city. The pink of an African dawn spread over the hilltops and down over the city, punctuated by the towers of the minarets. Hard not to believe that there is a God in his heaven at a time like this.

The Merenids ruled Fez at its zenith, which coincided with the richest period for trans-Saharan trade. It became the capital of Morocco and a world centre for Islam and learning. They embarked on a massive public works programme, building madrassas (religious schools), foundouqs, mosques, drinking fountains and palaces.

Their motives, however, were not entirely altruistic. When they conquered Fez, they faced a lot of opposition from the religious establishment who wielded significant power. They saw the Merenids as uneducated, uncultured, just-off-the-farm upstarts. By building the madrassas and providing the students with small grants and free bed and board, they won over the religious teachers and bred whole generations of loyal scholars.

The madrassas are important to our story because they attracted students from across West Africa who helped spread Islam across the Sahara. Knowledge and learning became one of the commodities traded from Fez down to Timbuktu, and up into Europe. Books and manuscripts joined salt and gold in terms of value and desirability.

The largest madrassa in Fez is the Bou Inania, built by Sultan Abou Inan. It is not too much of a stretch to imagine that he built it to appease the Lord, as Abou Inan was, by all accounts, quite a transgressor. Legend has it that in ten years, he managed to father 325 sons, depose his father and commit a series of unusually atrocious murders. In fact, the religious leaders advised him to build his madrassa on the city's rubbish dump on the basis that good works can cure anything. Money was no object and he spent so much on it that when he got the accounts he threw them into the river saying, "A thing of beauty is beyond reckoning." In the end, he got his own reckoning and was strangled by order of his First Minister.

Learning went down to Timbuktu from Fez but it also went up and across to Europe. At a time when Europe was languishing in the Dark Ages, Islam was enjoying a golden age, leading the world in research on medicine, mathematics, chemistry, biology and law. The astrolabe, for example, had its roots in classical Greece with Hipparchus, but was refined and used widely by the Islamic world and the oldest existing ones are Arab dating from the tenth century. They then went back into Europe. They were particularly precious to Islam as they allowed muslims to determine the astrologically defined prayer times and also the direction of Mecca, which is the direction you have to pray to.

We headed back down into the medina to search out some more clues to Timbuktu. They didn't take long to unearth. We had wanted to film at the shrine of Sidi Ahmed Tijani, a sufi saint. He had completely memorised the Quran by the age of seven and went on to give out his first fatwa when he was just fifteen. He also spent long periods meditating in the Sahara desert. He gathered a large group of disciples around him who disseminated his teachings along the old trade routes and he still has millions of followers in West Africa. In fact, many West Africans still stop off at his shrine in Fez as the first stage of their pilgrimage to Mecca.

As non-muslims, we aren't allowed in to any mosques or shrines in Morocco, so had to content ourselves with the activity at the doors. The Tijani bookshop opposite the shrine seemed a good place to start and I spotted three colourfully dressed West African women looking through the books. I bounced up to them to ask them if they would talk to us, but no amount of pleading made any impression and it was a firm no. Laura had more luck. She has chased down a tall, young Senegalese man. He agrees to be filmed doing his ablutions at the water fountain, "But only if the water is not too cold, I am frightened of the cold water." Afterwards we have a chat and I find out that he is in Fez studying Arabic sharia law. I explain that I too studied Arabic and we have a mutual admiration moment at the quality of our classical language. So many times on this journey, the past and the present merged. Five hundred years ago, Mansa Musa sent hundreds of young men up to study Islam in Fez. My new friend was doing the same thing all these centuries later.

Getting shots of the shrine takes a long time so I am free to wander around. I watch a woman who is sitting outside and has one new big pink blanket to sell. She gets some interest but no takers. At one point, a man selling white plastic shoes tries to do a trade. Lots of back and forth but still no trade. Everyone is very friendly and curious as to what we are doing. When I explain about the programme they ask me earnestly to make sure we do a good job, and give a good account of Morocco.

Midday in the medina is hectic. It is crowded with shoppers, traders, donkeys carrying toppling loads of vegetables and mattresses and we are having a hard time filming through the narrow alleyways. Some carters go past us shouting, "Make way, make way." Séamas asks our carter, Mohammed, who is now firmly one of the team, to do the same. He embraces the new challenge with fervour and before we know it we have picked up speed and are trotting behind him as he careers through pedestrians, scattering them to left and right.

The University of Al Karaouine makes the Guinness Book of Records as the oldest existing, continually operating and first degree awarding educational institution in the world – the oldest university in fact. It was founded by a female immigrant, Fatima Al Fihri, in 859. She was the well-educated daughter of a merchant who had brought his family to Fez from Tunisia and she built the mosque, a madrassa and founded the library which still houses over 4000 manuscripts including a 9th century Quran. The university still specialises in Islam and Islamic jurisprudence and classes are taught in the traditional way, sitting around one of the pillars in the courtyard.

We've crammed a huge amount of filming into one morning, but Alicia, the shot monster, always wants just one more shot and chats to Charlie about moving round the schedule.

"Charlie's giving me looks," she says.

"I'm giving you evils!" he replies.

Our aim was to get the train and zip down to our next big stop on the route, Marrakech. But things were not looking good. Everywhere you film in Morocco, you need a film permit and for the train you need lots of different ones including the city of Fez, the railway station, the train itself, Marrakech railway station… you get the picture. The bad news for us, was that our permits still hadn't come through and our train was due at 2.40. Toby had been despatched to Rabat where he was sitting in the Ministry. Charlie's ear had gone slightly red from holding the phone to it. We head to the station where it had just started to rain lightly. We all stand around disconsolately as 2.40 comes and goes.

"I've just looked at the weather forecast for Marrakech," says Séamas, "and it's bad. "Why don't we just stay where we are for the night and do the train tomorrow."

That gives us half a day's rest. We all agree to take it today and give a full one up later. Fez has been intense.

"I suggest you start your rest day ASAP," says Charlie, "as we are actually already at 3pm."

"But we need a hotel," says Laura.

"There's one," says Charlie and points to the Ibis across the car park.

Joy breaks out. The Ibis! Guaranteed electricity, soft bed and hot shower. We rampage across the car park, lug all the camera equipment into Séamas' room and head gratefully for our own. Laura spent her time on Netflix and logging, Séamas with the latest Edna O'Brien and me stressing out about how to get better at doing pieces to camera, having a very long shower and a far too short nap.

The next day, permits attained we board the Marrakech Express and head for my home city and I hummed snatches of the Crosby, Stills and Nash song, "The Marrakech Express". It was a song of the sixties when Marrakech was a must-do stop off on the hippie trail. It was written by Graham Nash when he took the train from Casablanca to Marrakech.

"There were a lot of older, rich American ladies in there, who all had their hair dyed blue," he recalled. "And I quickly grew bored of that and went back to the third class of the train. That was where it was all happening. There were lots of people cooking strange little meals on wooden stoves and the place was full of chickens and pigs and goats. It was fabulous. The whole thing was fabulous."

Nowadays, there's no cooking or animals but it is still a great place to meet people. While we are filming on the platform, I see three young Moroccan women in one of the carriages. They are smiling and blowing kisses at us, so obviously film friendly. I ask if I can sit with them and start to get to know them. All three of them are student nurses in their first year. If you have a stereotype of what a young, Muslim woman is like in Morocco, Fatima Zahra probably isn't it. Impeccably made up, with a Liverpool brow, a blue puffer jacket and a white beret, she made me feel slightly silly in my tunic and scarf. She told me that she was 23, had a three year old son and was divorced. Divorce is still relatively unacceptable in Morocco.

"I fell down," she told me, "but then I got up again. Everything I do is for my son. I learn for him, I work for him." I am pretty sure her son will be very proud of her in the future. She was obviously a strong-minded woman but she still had her anxieties.

"I don't look like a mother do I? I don't look old?" I reassured her that she looked beautiful and when the girls' stop came up, we grabbed some quick selfies, kissed and said goodbye.

Head on the window, I watched the rain pelt down, turning the brown earth to mud, and started dreaming of the Sahara and the heat of the desert. Now though, it was time for Marrakech, my adopted city, my home and the other great trading post of Morocco. In terms of our route, Fez and Marrakech are where so much of the actual buying and selling of goods was done on this road between sub-Saharan Africa and Europe.

"The red city, the ochre city, the daughter of the desert." I love Marrakech. I've been living here for three years and the honeymoon period is still going strong. In the winter, you can see the snow-topped Atlas mountains in the distance. Roses grow in profusion all along the main boulevards and when you enter the red walls of the medina, you are stepping straight into Africa. There are Malian women sitting in the main square selling wooden giraffes, old cowries are jumbled in with the second hand junk spread on rugs and handsome young Senegalese boys come up with Rolexes and offers of sex. "You want a big dick, Lady?"

 The Marrakchis are a cheerful bunch, always ready to have a chat and share a joke until they get behind the wheel of a car or onto a moto, when they transform into road monsters. In spring, the orange trees blossom and you catch snatches of the perfume everywhere you go. It is a town of salesmen, artists, beggars and tour guides. Don't expect a quiet stroll through the medina, no, you will be assailed at every turn with people wanting to sell you something and "just have a look" rarely means that. But they are only doing their jobs, and if you have the time and a smile, it's a pleasure rather than a hassle. I like the fact that I can go for a wander to the old spice market with its mounds of cumin, cinnamon and star anise, and then take a horse and carriage back to my neighbourhood to sit in a French café for an expresso.

Charlie describes it perfectly.

"It's got that feel to it. It's an oasis and a trading town. It's got its roots in trade and sub-Saharan Africa. It gets its influences from the south whereas Fez gets them from the east. It is so diverse and cosmopolitan but still traditional. You can see medieval street scenes and then be in a very sophisticated boutique guest house."

I was excited to get the chance to show some of this off on film so awoke on day one in Marrakech full of optimism. The tortoise and cats were glad to see me back too. Although, Mumu, the tortoise was in semi-hibernation and a bit dopey. First stop was something I had been looking forward to. I was going to spend a morning working in one of the tanneries, helping to clean and cure the animal hides.

Marrakech has transformed beyond all recognition and yet not changed at all since the days when merchants brought their caravans in to the city to trade in every type of goods imaginable. It still makes its money through trade and being a hub for travellers. Everyone here is a craftsman. Along with a fantastic ability to pick up languages, it seems to be the genetic heritage of the Marrakchi. Leather workers, wood workers, weavers, embroiderers, silversmiths can all be found tucked away in different corners of the medina.

Leather goods have always been one of the biggest sellers and I was there in the tannery to do my bit for Moroccan trade. It was chilly, so I stopped off for a bowl of salty porridge being cooked and sold by a woman at the gate. She had a circle of hungry workers around her, sitting on tiny stools. Cost me 30 pence.

The full fragrance of the tannery hit me as we went up to meet my co-workers and tannery teachers, Naguib and Mohammed. The dress code was old and disposable. I was given long rubber waders. Naguib tenderly wrapped my feet in plastic bags first and then helped me pull them on. I also had cloth gloves followed by rubber gauntlets.

The whole tanning process is complex and involves many different stages. I got to experience some of them. First of all, we salted the skins and then pulled the hair off with our hands and rinsed. Great clumps of it came out with every scrub.

Next stage was to get into one of the vats to start trampling the hides. The vats were filled with a murky grey liquid that smelt like hell, or at least like sulphur and something else nasty. It was made up of water and pigeon shit. Nice! The acid from the pigeon shit helps cure the hides. I also heard the words quicklime and poison. I was slightly alarmed by the poison. However, Naguib and Mohammed leapt in, I leapt in, and then, oops, I realised that I was not as tall as they were. Grey pigeon shit water was running down my thighs and into my boots. My waders were filling up.

Agh! I flailed around torn between horror and hilarity.

"Naguib, Naguib get me out of here!". Thank goodness for upper body strength, the pair of them hauled me out of the tub, squelchy and pongy.

No rest for the wicked and onto a shallower tub, filled with the same delightful mixture. There we stomped around in a circle, creating a whirlpool. The combination of the hides winding around your legs and the current we had created made it hard physical work. I tried to imagine doing it in the heat of the summer when Marrakech hits 48 degrees, or doing it when I was fasting for Ramadan and couldn't even have a drink of water.

My thighs were burning when we went on to the next tub where we had to drag the hides, rinsing them by making them into a kind of balloon through the water. Mohammed tried to teach me: two thumbs on the hide, swish it through the water, turn it inside out and then scrape off the fatty residue and hair. I was useless but did manage to amuse myself by sticking my finger through what had been my little goat's bumhole. The men were focussed on their task and, TV or no TV, had their hides to get through, so used me as a junior labourer. I felt like part of the team, and just did what I was told.

One of the latter stages sounded very romantic. The hides are soaked in mimosa to strengthen them and start to neutralise the smell. I will never think of mimosa in the same way.

The tannery was over a thousand years old, so would have been operating and supplying leather for the sub-Saharan trade, and the methods of curing the hides were unchanged, that sense of history again.

Before I met Naguib and Mohammed, I had always felt pity for the tanners, because the job is so tough and the conditions are harsh. But Naguib put me straight. He was fiercely proud of his craft.

He had been working there for 48 years. As a schoolboy he used to come after school and in the holidays.

"Our grandfathers, our ancestors and before them and before them worked here, it goes back to a distant history. It feeds our children, gives us everything," he told me as we said goodbye. "Don't forget to come to work tomorrow. Eight o'clock."

As we are walking back through the suq towards Jema El Fna, the main square, we pass lots of shops crammed with all colours of leather slippers, shops which in a few months could be selling slippers made from the leather I helped cure. Laura breaks into my reverie.

"Did you know the yellow slippers are dyed with pomegranates? That is what makes them that colour."

A fantastic fact. I feel a piece to camera coming on.

Jema El Fna is Marrakech's heart. It is the gathering place for the whole city and at night it can reach bursting point as Moroccans and tourists come down to watch the acrobats and snake charmers, take pictures with the water sellers in their red hats, fish for fanta bottles, eat at the local food stalls and listen to the traditional story tellers. That is what we are going to do, as we know there is one story teller who specialises in tales of trade from days of yore. We have a couple of hours to kill though and the weather has taken a turn for the worse.

When I signed up for this TV programme, I hadn't thought much about what I would wear. If anything, I thought it would be walking trousers and boots and a shirt and fleece with my nice cosy down jacket for when it was cold. How naïve I was. What I would wear was a major issue and caused me major grief. It was decided that I should reflect the fact that I lived in Marrakech and so a tunic, trousers and scarf was agreed. That was fine by me as I am very happy to waft about in a kaftan during the summer when it is hot and a tunic was on the same lines. However, I didn't factor in how hard it would be to find the right tunic. This is too long and dull a story to recount but involved many false starts, a lot of angst-ridden phone calls and trying on of hideous clothes and final rescue by Alicia who came up absolutely trumps. We called it Tunicgate. I also didn't factor in waiting around for hours in the freezing cold and rain.

"Yep," said Alicia, "This is the sad reality of television. There is always an awful lot of waiting around." I eyed her in her puffer jacket and boots with some rancour. I was wearing my tunic, a scarf, thin trousers and flimsy shoes. An hour later and my temper had gone from grumpy to frozen despair. My nice façade, that I felt I had been doing a really good job keeping up, shattered. I was very, very cold and very, very cross. Most annoying was the thought that if I had had some foresight I could have brought a warm jacket and pair of Ugg boots from home to wear while we were waiting. Fed up with my own ill humour, I went off into the suq to buy something warm and found what came to be known as the emergency jellaba (kaftan), a rather fetching concoction in pink tweed with a hood and a look of Chanel. It only cost me £4.00 so I felt I had a bargain. My mood plummeted again though when I had to take it off to walk round the square for some night time shots with the wind whistling round me and my shoes coming apart in the puddles. Laura had to be dispatched over to tell me to amend my facial expression.

I cheered up when we met our storyteller, though. A group of Marrakchis had gathered at his spot as he launched in to his fabulous tale. This man was a master of his art. He didn't speak loudly or use lots and lots of gestures or any props but he had us all in his thrall. Storytelling is another tradition that has survived for hundreds of years and the merchants of old would have done exactly what I was doing and settled down to be entertained.

"Heat was coming from the top and the bottom, the sun was burning, the sand as well. Even the stored water was beginning to dry out from the heat." Si Mohammed wove us a tale of courage, greed, thirst, gold, mountains of salt and trading fortunes won and lost. He took us from Tangier to Timbuktu but ended in Morocco, the land of plenty. When he had finished, there was tumultuous applause and lots of questions. Tea was handed round and after he was thanked by the host, I was asked to propose a toast.

"To Morocco!" I said. "To Morocco, thanks be to God!" was the reply.

I wanted to get to know a little bit more about Si Mohammed and storytelling. This is what he told me.

"Back in 1959 when I first started, I started with "One thousand and One Nights". There are actually two types of stories; the ones written in books, and the ones we heard from other story tellers. These stories are passed throughout the generations. Our grandfathers and grandmothers used to gather us around to listen to them before we went to sleep. There was no television back then, no radio, no satellite, nothing. Stories were the only entertainment available.

"Story tellers then were known as entertainers, and were an indispensible means of entertainment to everyone – to the royals as well.

"Stories vary. There are love stories of couples having to go through ups and downs before they can finally be together. There are stories of evil people who finally get punished by God. There are war stories that tell about fighters and soldiers and many other kinds of stories. We, the story tellers, must actually know all these kinds of stories.

"Every time you tell a story, you look for a new one, you must always have new stories to tell, and you must always be in search. But also people may actually ask you to tell a certain story, and you are expected to know it!"

I wondered what our story of tracing these routes with history and the present constantly colliding would end up as. We were leaving the big cosmopolitan trading centres of Fez and Marrakech behind us now to head up and out to the mountains and the first big physical barrier of the route, the Atlas.

Chapter Three

"I set out alone, having neither fellow traveler in whose companionship I might find cheer nor caravan whose party I might join but swayed by an overmastering impulse within me and a desire long-cherished in my bosom to visit these illustrious sanctuaries."

Ibn Battuta, Al Rihla, 1353

Two intractable obstacles lie between Timbuktu and Europe. Hostile terrains on the opposite end of the scale from each other. The Atlas Mountains and the Sahara Desert. One freezing cold, high altitude, with a risk of blizzards in the winter and flash floods in the summer. The other burning hot, with no water, no food and no hope of rescue if your supplies ran out.

This leg of our journey was across the first of those, the mighty Atlas. The Atlas Mountains stretch over about 2500km through Tunisia, Algeria and Morocco and house North Africa's highest peak, Mount Toubkal, at 4167 metres.

They are much more than statistics to me, though. In fact, I fell in love with Morocco in the Atlas Mountains. I remember years ago, looking at hiking holidays in the Atlas and thinking to myself, "Why would you ever go on holiday there, it's bound to be really barren and a bit boring." As I have been many times before, I was totally wrong. My first few days hiking through the peaks, walking into tiny Berber villages clinging to the rock faces and smelling juniper on the breeze and I was totally hooked. A year later and I moved to Morocco to live. I dream of hiking them from end to end one day.

The myth is that they are called the Atlas Mountains after the Titan, Atlas, who was condemned to hold up the sky for eternity after the Titans lost the battle against the Olympians over who would be gods of the universe. The Atlas Mountains are said to hold up the sky over Africa. More prosaically, the name probably comes from a corruption of the Berber word for mountains which is Adrar or Adras.

Our aim was to get a feel of what it would have been like for the merchants, crossing the range with their goods. We were crossing in November and so there was already plenty of snow underfoot and the threat of more on the way which would threaten our ability to climb up and over the peak. Glorious weather though, with the sky dazzlingly blue and the sun out.

Saaid Naanaa (which translates as Happy Mint!) had agreed to guide us up and over and he is a friend of old so I was excited to see him again. He is a hiking guide but also an excellent biker and leads mountain bike and road bike tours. There were quite a lot of logistics to consider for this stage as the filming equipment is heavy and unwieldy and we wouldn't have access to a road which meant us carrying it.

We met Saaid at a village at the end of the piste. I was immediately invited in for tea by a Berber lady. Her house was built of stone and compacted mud and was spotlessly clean. There was minimal furniture, just some stools and hard banquettes which doubled as beds and seats. She was cooking porridge on the stove and was churning milk in her kitchen. The churn was very ingenuous. It was a blue, plastic barrel hung between two ropes which she could swing back and forth.

Outside, there was a communal bread oven, with the fire roaring and a group of women clustered around. One of them had the most beautiful green eyes, and her daughter had eyelashes that would have made Elizabeth Taylor envious. Did you know that Elizabeth Taylor had a double row of eyelashes naturally? One woman had a thorn in her thumb and her friend was trying to squeeze it out. Her hands were beautifully hennaed and I asked her if she had been to a wedding as that is normally why people get their hands decoratively hennaed. Women in the mountains regularly completely cover the soles of their feet and the palms of their hands in henna to strengthen them as it is thought to toughen up the skin. Some Moroccan male ultra runners do it too, to try and keep their feet from blistering. In this case, she told me she had just had it done to, "look beautiful for my family." Watched by the chickens and the goats, quite a crowd had gathered to see what we were up to in the village square. Naturally, everyone was happy to have a chat about what we were doing and proffer advice on the route and the best way to carry the gear.

Séamas and Alicia decided to take just the big camera and a smaller one, and the extra batteries and bits were distributed. I had the easy job. All I had to do was walk and talk to Saaid. As we set off, we met the primary school class coming in the opposite direction. When the teacher saw us, she got them all to start singing a French song in our honour. It was one of those moments. The children singing like little birds under a bright blue sky, with snow underfoot and the high peaks all around.

We were heading up and over the Tischka pass. These routes are still only accessible by foot and mule, just as they used to be. Camels aren't used in the High Atlas because their pads slip and aren't suitable for the narrow, rocky paths. I do wonder how Hannibal got his elephants over the alps. Mules are called Berber 4x4s in Morocco (assardoun or tassardount for a female) in Tashlaheet, the Berber language for this area. The females are more valuable because they last longer, are more reliable and have better tempers. All the women in our group enjoyed this nugget of information.

The people of the High Atlas are primarily Berbers who speak Tashlaheet. The language is totally different from Arabic and has been mainly an oral one but a new alphabet was recently compiled and introduced and it was made an official language in Morocco. The alphabet can be read both left to right like English and also top to bottom.

For some, the name Berber, is actually insulting as the correct word is Amazigh (singular) or Imazighen (plural) which means the Free Men. The word Berber came from the ancient Greek barbaros and was used to describe anyone who didn't speak Greek – bar bar are nonsense syllables like blah blah. It was then used by the Romans to describe the hostile hordes they faced in the northern territories including the Gauls and the Celts. The Arabs also used the word Al Barbar when they swept across North Africa in the seventh century. So, it is easy to see why the Imazighen might prefer to be called by their real name.

The Imazighen are spread across the whole of Northern Africa from Morocco, where they make up around 40% of the population, through Algeria, Tunisia and to Egypt. They are also in Mauritania, Mali and Niger. They provided the great dynasties of Moroccan rulers right up until the 16th century and Imazighen soldiers were the backbone of the Arab army that invaded Spain at the time of the conquest.

Islam is the predominant religion now, but there used to be large Jewish communities of Imazighen Moroccans. It was also the Imazighen who dominated the trans Saharan trade and forged the trade routes between Africa and Europe.

Subsistence agriculture in the mountains and herding were the mainstay of the economy and remains so today, along with the more modern trade of tourism. It is impossible to generalise about a whole people but I have noticed some distinct traits amongst the Imazighen in the mountains after spending a lot of time there. Women do not hide away or shy from meeting strangers and joining in social discourse, even with foreign men. In fact,they often lead it. The people are also much kinder to their animals. I have never seen an ill-treated or ill-kept mule or donkey in the hills, as opposed to in the cities where brutality is commonplace. The last thing is very hard to characterise, but finds its expression in a kind of spirituality. Perhaps because of the magnificent mountain and desert landscapes that surround them, the people are very in tune with nature and tie it in to their religious life. One of the best things about coming into an Amazigh village at the end of a long day's walking, is when you pass little groups of people sitting on a rock or in a field, chatting and laughing and enjoying the evening together.

Saaid is Amazigh and comes from a semi-Nomadic family. The muleteers and mountain guides for the traders would also have been Imazighen. He led us up and up. The going was nice and testing. The snow and altitude added a challenge and there were some steep, slippery descents to navigate. We had to keep the pace up as we needed to make the pass before dark. This part of the mountains was not the place to be navigating after dark with ice underfoot and sheer fallaways to the side, with nothing to stop you for hundreds of metres. Incomprehensible to me how a fully laden mule could pass this way, but Saaid assured me that they would be able to do so as long as the route didn't become icy. Then, they would have to take a different path.

We were chatting as we walked and came to a flattish plateau with plenty of snow. I wanted Saaid to show the others the Amazigh symbol and he obligingly drew it for them. It looks like a man with his arms upstretched and his legs spread and it represents freedom. Saaid showed us that it is initially drawn as a diagonal line with two semi circles – one above and one below. These semi circles represent chains. When you break them, what emerges is a man standing with his arms reaching out. This is also the symbol for the last letter of the alphabet. It is the centre of the Amazigh flag and is coloured red to represent life and also resistance. The other colours on the flag are blue for the sea, green for nature and the mountains and yellow for the desert, together it shows people living in harmony with the land.

The biggest obstacle we had to overcome during this part of the journey was crossing the rivers and waterfalls that plunged down, fuelled by snowmelt. We had done a couple of minor ones with no mishaps and just had one big one to do before a push up to the main peak.

Saaid found us the best place to cross. The river was coming down from a waterfall and was moving very fast. The place we were going to cross was flattish with some big rocks that weren't quite steppable, you needed to jump. Saaid took up his position at the edge of the opposite bank, ready to reach his hand across.

Charlie and Séamas leapt across, followed by Laura and Alicia. Then it was my turn. Now, I do a lot of hiking in these mountains, but I am not a big fan of rivers. I never feel able to trust the rocks and just jump. I am always sure I am going to slip and fall. I prefer to dig in my poles if possible and lever myself gingerly over, usually while shrieking. I know that that is not very impressive from someone who calls themselves an Adventurer, but there it is. I approached with caution, like a cat but without the feline grace. Saaid straddled the rocks and reached out his hand.

"Just jump Alice, it's not difficult."

"I'm going to slip, Saaid. I don't like it."

"No, it's fine. Honestly, it's fine. Just jump." .

"No, seriously, I'm not joking. I'm not going to make it. I'm going to fall in."

I jumped. I fell in up to my waist in freezing snow melt. Saaid's walking pole floated down the river to Marrakech. Séamas looked up at me from his camera with a happy smile, "I had a good feeling when I stepped across that river."

The rest of the hike was accomplished with a soaking wet bottom and legs, but that didn't hurt nearly as much as my pride.

We crested the main Tischka Pass, and came abruptly out of the wilderness and into a car park. We had joined up with the main road between Marrakech and the south, where the trade now is in tourists. It was icy on the top and those burning sands of the Sahara glimmered tantalisingly in front of me in my imagination. It did underline how short the trading season would have been. We were passing in November and the route was already becoming snowbound and would remain so until March. In the summer months, the desert is virtually impassable as temperatures go into the fifties. The merchants would have had to choose their times in Spring and Autumn.

That night we stayed in a local guest house in Tazga which Charlie had found. We had driven down there in the pitch black and in sub-zero temperatures. It was in the middle of nowhere on a piste and we stopped a few times to ask directions at local houses. We were cold and tired.

"I hope the guest house is nice," said Alicia.

Charlie was silent.

"All I want is for it to be warm and to have a good shower," said Alicia.

Charlie was silent.

"I'm going to wash my hair. I hope they have a hairdryer," said Alicia

Charlie was silent.

We arrived at the guest house which lay in an orchard criss-crossed by irrigation channels. There was no light pollution and the Milky Way shone clearly. Alicia forged ahead ready for all her dreams to come true, eager for that hot shower and hairdryer.

Her dreams shattered, just like the ice on the windows. It was colder inside than out, of course there was no hot water and as for a hairdryer… But Alicia did get put in a Moroccan Disney princess room, with a four-poster bed draped all in blue and a myriad of spangles and cushions. Our hosts were completely charming and hot mint tea helped with the thaw. A fire was burning in the main room and we all begged gaffer tape from Séamas so we could tape our wet stuff up above it. The fragrant scent of steaming sock filled the air. I finally got my wet clothes off and put on every other single thing I owned, including the emergency jellaba. Alicia debated whether to try out the cold shower, which seemed like an exercise in foolhardiness to me, anyway I was clean from my river bath. Dinner made up for everything as the owner had cooked us some real local delicacies including a quince and hare tagine.

At first light, I got up and went out to see where we were, as we had arrived in the dark. Right opposite the orchard was a ruined Kasbah and stretching along the valley I could see the outline of more. The Kasbahs were fortified houses on the old trade routes so we were clearly on track. The early morning light picked out every rock and blade of grass in the valley and a tiny bird just like a robin but with a yellow breast came up and kept me company while I enjoyed it.

The reason we were staying at that particular guest house was that the family also owned the next place on our journey. The salt mine. This was our second big clue on the route to Timbuktu. Gold had been our first. Trade had been in salt and gold and slaves and the routes had been created specifically to transport these most valuable of commodities. This salt mine had been producing salt for centuries and it was bang on the route.

Morocco is such a land of contrasts. The day before I had been hiking up a snow-covered mountain and now I was walking through a red-stoned gorge, with a small stream flowing down it. The colours were vivid. Blue, blue sky above and red, red earth on each side. Red underfoot too until I got a bit further in, where it turned to crystal white. Salt residue had hardened along the path of the stream and formed white crystals, crunchy when I walked on them. I stopped off to break the ice on a water trough and wash my face.

The entrance to the mine was through a door in the side of the hill, just like a hobbit door. The guardian saw me coming and ran over from his hut with a big, iron key just as the owner, Zac, drove up. The key turned gratifyingly loudly in the lock and the door creaked open. I ducked my head down and followed Zac in. The guardian had a lantern and by its light I could see a big cavernous space and feel the warmth coming from the earth. Then Zac turned the torch on. A vaulted ceiling, covered in twinkling salt stars soared above me. In the far reaches I could see water sparkling and the floor was covered in glinting crystals. A fairy tale. I knew that at one point in trading history, salt and gold were traded kilo for kilo. But, for the first time in this gleaming, hidden place I could feel that salt really was a treasure.

"The mine was situated on the route of the caravans. And it was one of the things they used to barter with, and they took with them when they left for Africa. They took the salt and returned with gold and slaves. The caravaneers from here, the Berbers and Arabs, they didn't leave from here, they came from the north.. the big imperial cities of Fez and Marrakech, they came with their merchandise and crossed the mountains, the mountain of Telouet and, when they crossed the pass of Telouet, it was a stage, a crossroads, on the route that goes directly to Mali and the south, it's a route that goes down the Ounila valley and then along the Draa and all the places all the way to Timbuktu. " Zac told me.

"The salt was a currency of the time, because it was the only way to preserve animals. There were no fridges, there were no generators."

Now, the salt is extracted by dynamite and I could see the areas of the wall where explosives had been placed but it used to be mined by men with pick axes, local villagers and also slaves who had been brought across the Sahara. Descendants of the miners and the slaves still live in the village close to the mine.

What I didn't realise is that there were different qualities of salt, mined in different ways. The good grade salt for trade would have been pick axed from the wall in big slabs about a metre high and half a metre wide with a depth of twenty centimetres. This salt was very

51

valuable and highly prized. Once it had been cleaned down, each bar would weigh upwards of eighty pounds and you would fit four of these onto every camel in your camel train. These blocks of salt were virtually indestructible and could survive the rigours of the journey to come. The good quality salt would then be used for preserving and flavouring food.

The leavings from the big slabs, were all over the ground of the cave. This salt is also bought and sold. It is much cheaper and is used for animal feed. There were also two other types of salt visible in the mine. One was the salt flowers on the roof, perfect white blooms and the other was salt crystallised at the edges of the underground lake. Both of these types, Zac explained, were deposits left when water flowed down through the mountain and were excellent quality.

They all looked different too, both in texture and colour. The lake salt was pure white and came off in long flakes, while the animal salt from the ground was a browner colour and had a more solid structure. Where the slabs were hewn from, the salt looked more like white or clear marble. All of them tasted salty, but I am afraid to say that, to me, all of them tasted the same, in spite of Zac's earnest entreaties to taste the difference.

"It's back to the salt mines." I am pretty sure I have actually said that, when all I was doing was returning to my desk in a nice office after a large Americano. Leaving the mine, fantasy and reality were warring in my head. I was enchanted by the magic of the mine but I knew that the salt miners' lives must have been very harsh, working in the heart of the mountain, gouging great blocks of salt down with their pickaxes. Wages would have been low and the hours long. If they got injured, there would have been no modern medicine to help them, and salt would have been rubbed into the cracks in their hands and feet as they worked. Then loading up the camels with the heavy slabs, securing all the ropes to try and minimise any saddle sores, and starting the great trek down across the Sahara and all its dangers to Timbuktu. Many of the workers would have been slaves, bound into a cycle of work, eat, sleep with no control over their lives or chance to make their own future. Many, taken away from their families, with no chance of ever seeing or speaking to them again.

Zac had begun to tell us a little of the story of the slaves in Morocco.

"In ancient Morocco, there were three classes in society, free men, haritan and slaves. Haritan comes from the words hurr (free) and thani (two) and it was a second stage between slaves and free men," he explained.

Generations ago, his family had owned slaves who had worked in the mines and today, descendants of those slaves still worked with his family. They all lived together in the nearby village. In fact, the man who had served us dinner the night before in the guest house was the great grandson of a slave which felt extraordinary.

The Ounila Valley is sometimes called the Valley of the Kasbahs, and it forms part of the old caravan route between the Sahara and Marrakech via the Draa Valley and the Tizi-n Telouet pass as described by Zac.

Kasbahs and ksars were central to the trade routes. A ksar is a fortified town or village with defensive walls complete with towers and patrolled by guards. The kasbah is a fortified house, a little bit like a castle, owned by the head man in that village and forms a corner stone of the ksar. The kasbah is a square building with turrets on each corner, made of thick, compacted mud walls. There is a central courtyard with rooms for people, animals and storage leading off it. Enormous reinforced wooden doors block the entrance and the whole thing is designed to be secure. The ksar incorporates the houses of the village, a well, a mosque, a public square and a place to thresh grain, foundouks for travelers and a Muslim cemetery. Some of the older ksars also have Jewish cemeteries.

The appeal to merchants is obvious. By staying in a kasbah, they could store their goods and animals overnight in complete security. Bandits would have to get through two sets of fortified walls and fight off the ksar guards. They also had all the amenities they would need- a mosque to pray in, food and drink for themselves and their animals and even a cemetery to be buried in if the worst should happen. Of course, they had to pay for the privilege and as a result the ksars on our trading route prospered and the kasbah owners became rich.

One of the most notorious was T'hami el Gelaoui, the ruler of Kasbah Telouet, the Pasha of Marrakech and the so-called Lord of the Atlas. The position of Kasbah Telouet couldn't be more perfect for successful warlording and accumulation of wealth. It is built overlooking the main trade route and very near to some large salt mines. Merchants travelling past would stay and pay or just give "gifts" to ensure a safe passage.

The story of El Gelouai goes like this.

El Gelaoui was the son of the ruler of Telouet and his beautiful Ethiopian concubine, Zora. When he was twenty years old, he and his brothers saved the sultan of Morocco from dying in a blizzard when he got stuck in the mountains during a tax gathering expedition. The grateful sultan presented the brothers with the very latest in military technology at that time – a 77-mm Krupp cannon. The brothers were delighted and immediately used the cannon to subdue all the rival warlords in the region.

El Gelaoui grew richer and richer and more and more powerful. He was legendarily generous with his money and a bit of a darling of the west. He attended Queen Elizabeth's coronation as a private guest of Winston Churchill. And Churchill is said to have often played on a golf course that El Gelaoui created in Marrakech. A warlord and a politician, he helped to topple two sultans and sided with the French colonisers, which earned him the hatred of many. When he died, he was the most powerful man in Morocco and one of the richest men in the world. His story is told in a book by Gavin Maxwell, "The Lord of the Atlas", well worth a read.

Perhaps the best known of the ksars to us nowadays is Ait Ben Haddou which has been immortalised in dozens of film and TV series. Do you remember Russell Crowe sweating it out in the ring as he trained to be a gladiator? It's certainly etched on my memory. That was filmed at Ait Ben Haddou. If you are more of a Daenerys fan, then cast your mind back to her conquest of the slave city of Yunkai, the yellow city. That is Ait Ben Haddou and if you visit you can stand in the exact spot where she refuses the city's gold, demanding slave freedom instead. When I was researching, I came across this brilliant factette on the Yunkai slaves.

"Yunkai is known for training bed slaves, not warriors. A slave in Yunkai learns the way of the seven sighs and the sixteen seats of pleasure. Yunkai can field an army of roughly five thousand men, all slaves. In Yunkai, eunuchs are made by only cutting the testicles off, unlike the Unsullied of Astapor.

Lucky old Yunkai eunuchs! And what are the ways of the seven sighs and the sixteen seats of pleasure?

As part of the story of the trade routes, we were keen to reflect what is happening now along these old ways. In Morocco, the economy is quite buoyant with around 3% growth. Exportingis still big business. Fruit and vegetables, grown in the south, are sent to the UK. Check your Tesco tomatoes, chances are they are from Morocco. Minerals are mined in the Atlas along with some silver and copper. There is a large garment industry based around Casablanca as well as the more bespoke leather and cloth goods that are sent abroad. Tourism, of course, plays a huge role as the country has so much to offer and is so close to Europe. And last but not least, film and TV play their part, taking advantage of all that places like Ait Ben Haddou have to offer. It really is big business in Morocco and that was our justification for slipping the film studios at Ouarzazate into the programme. I have to admit that my motivation was a desire to star as an extra in Game of Thrones or maybe The Night Manager 2, or Mission Impossible 6 and win undying fame. My imagination ran riot.

"TV filming basically consists of always being late and always having to apologise," was Laura's mantra. She was in charge of the schedule so was constantly having to urge us on to hurry. Alicia is a shot monster and always, always wants "just one more", so Laura did not have an easy task. She has the skills of a world-class diplomat and her apologies as we turned up an hour late for yet another contributor, would earn her a fortune as a celebrity PR person. I have had to say my fair share of sorrys to people and have always had a grain of fellow feeling for when the great and not so good have to grovel publicly. Favourites include the immortal one from Hugh Grant, when he was arrested after hooking up with Hollywood prostitute Divine Brown. He had this to say to Jay Leno on "The Tonight Show".

"You know in life what's a good thing to do and a what's a bad thing, and I did a bad thing. And there you have it," he told Leno.

Needless to say, we arrived at the film studios, where I was due to meet Mohammed Brad Pitt, a couple of hours behind schedule. I had no idea who he was as Laura and Alicia wanted it to be a surprise for me so that I could meet him when the viewer met him. In Laura's words "It's all about keeping the talent in the dark." I understood the concept but for a naturally nosey person, this was hell. Especially as I had been overhearing snippets of conversations all the way down the route.

"Wait till she meets Mohammed Brad Pitt."

"Mohammed Brad Pitt is going to be great."

"Mohammed Brad Pitt is a total star."

"He's a smooth kind of guy."

Anyway, my time was come. I was ready for my world to be rocked. I hoped the lateness wasn't going to matter to Mr Pitt.

Laura and Charlie went in to negotiate and I was dispatched to the toilets to change out of my striding around clothes and into my tunic and scarf combo – felt to be more suitable for swanning around a studio.

When I got back to the car, there was a cluster of annoyed faces and raised voices. For whatever reason, maybe because we were a bit later or maybe just because it was a Friday, the film studios had arbitrarily raised their location fee to a level that just didn't make any sense. Filming permits and location fees were the bane of Charlie's life as he navigated us through the country. Usually, there was a way around things. Bartering is, after all, a way of life here as anyone who has ever tried to find out the price of something in the Marrakech markets knows. But this time, there was no moving them, they were clearly used to larger production budgets. I was doomed to remain an undiscovered star and never to meet Mohammed Brad Pitt.

"Doesn't fit the story anyway," said Charlie as we drove off. He was right but I was still regretful.

As to Mohammed Brad Pitt, I found out that he was one of the studio guides and when I was shown a picture of him by Laura I could discover no similarity whatsoever. Kudos to him for a good sense of humour and an alarming sense of self worth!

The next day, we had the morning off to enjoy the glories of Ouarzazate, the gateway to the desert. I am fond of Ouarzazate because it is where you go after the Marathon des Sables finishes so it has lots of great memories. Dimitri's Greek restaurant is the place to eat. It is covered with signed pictures of the stars who have eaten there and inspired James, who has worked on over 80 filming jobs in Morocco, to a stream of movie-related anecdotes. Personal protection officer to Brad and Ang… I felt we were not quite worthy.

The contrast with our next stage would be very marked as we left civilization behind us and headed into the stone age scenery of the

Jebel Saghro to walk with nomads.

Chapter Four

"The Bedouins, on the other hand, live separately from the community. They are alone in the country and remote from militias. They have no walls and gates. Therefore, they provide their own defense and do not entrust it to, or rely upon others for it. They always carry weapons. They watch carefully all sides of the road. They take hurried naps only when they are together in company or when they are in the saddle. They pay attention to every faint barking and noise. They go alone into the desert, guided by their fortitude, putting their trust in themselves. Fortitude has become a character quality of theirs, and courage their nature. They use it whenever they are called upon or an alarm stirs them. When sedentary people mix with them in the desert or associate with them on a journey, they depend on them. They cannot do anything for themselves without them."

Ibn Khaldun – Al Muqaddima

I search for words to try and describe the Jebel Saghro. Prehistoric, primeval, ancient, stone age, lunar pop into my head but I am not sure they are quite right. Magnificent, awe-inspiring, humbling also apply but they are a bit inadequate too. It is one of my favourite regions in Morocco and one that, if you get a chance, you should visit.

Geographically, it is a mountain range, south of the High Atlas and east of the Anti-Atlas lying to the southwest of Ouarzazate. It is actually an eastern prolongation of the Anti-Atlas range, sandwiched between the valley of the Draâ and the Dadès valley in the north which separates it from the High Atlas we had just crossed.

Jebel means mountain and Saghro in the Tamazight language, one of the three Amazigh languages spoken in Morrocco, means drought. The area is aptly named as it is the driest mountain area of the whole Atlas mountains. It does not get the Atlantic Ocean winds that bring water to the Anti-Atlas ranges further to the west, so annual rainfall is only 100 mm on the southern slopes and 300 mm at the summits. Contrast that with Ben Nevis where you get 4350 mm at the top and 2050mm at the bottom and it gives you some idea of how dry it is. In the Highlands, it is sheep that graze the rain-drenched slopes but in the Jebel Saghro the main livestock is goats as they fare better, although sheep are herded too.

The highest summit of the range is only 2,712 m high which is nowhere near the 4000 m plus summits of the High Atlas, but its lunar landscape of vast empty plains punctuated by volcanic plugs of rock catapulted out of the earth make it just as dramatic.

The Jebel Saghro area is the traditional homeland of the Aït Atta tribe. The Aït Atta were the last tribe in Morocco to hold out against the French and, in the end, were only defeated when the French brought in air power, a technology they had no chance of combatting from horse and camel back. Very few people can scrape out a living in the Saghro and many of those that do live in the region are nomads, moving with the seasons and searching for any pasture they can find in this arid place.

As part of this quest for Timbuktu I wanted to get closer to the life that was lived all those years ago and experience it as viscerally as possible. So, we were here to walk with the nomads whose lifestyle remains virtually unchanged from centuries past.

Our host was Zaid from the Ait Atta, his mother Aisha, wife Izza, daughters Zara (14) and little Aisha (3), sons Mohammed (16), Maymoun, Hassan and baby Brahim (2) and finally young Zaid who was either a nephew or a cousin, I couldn't quite get the hang of it. Two and a half years ago I had been lucky enough to spend a week walking with the family on their annual migration. Every year they trek for two weeks to the high pastures of the Atlas Mountains with their flocks. They stay there all summer, feeding up the goats, and then walk back in September. It was one of those experiences that had stayed etched in my mind.

We had set off with 210 goats, 1 sheep, 7 mules, 10 camels, 3 donkeys, 2 dogs, 22 people and one chicken and walked only as fast as the animals would allow, given that they had to graze on route. One of my abiding memories was of Zara, who had been around 12 at the time. She had been shy with me all week but I had been working on her and finally near the end of the trip when I spent the whole day herding with her and her Mum, rather than with the caravan, I got to see her in her element. She was constantly alert for what the goats were doing but she was smiling and laughing and even got brave enough to tease me by calling me Tamkhilawt – the mad one. At one point in the day I lost her and wasn't sure where she had disappeared to, then she popped over a hill crest and came skipping down. She reached into her pocket and brought out a beautiful white crystallized rock she had found on the trail as a present. I still have it as a reminder of all the really good things in life.

I had been looking forward to this part of the trip with unalloyed pleasure. I couldn't wait for the others to see the Jebel Saghro and I was eager to spend time with the family again. That experience of walking and living in an unchanged way, in an unchanged landscape is incredibly precious. What I hadn't bargained for was the culture clash that would ensue when we introduced TV and its needs into the mix. My lack of experience had made me an optimist, a foolish one.

I arrived at the camp, one hundred per cent ready to immerse myself in the past, so it was a bit of a culture shock to be met by an ultra cool French guy called Sebastien, who looked a bit like a rock star complete with boots. He was our drone pilot and a long-term resident of Casablanca. Tern TV had hired him to do some drone shots so that we could capture the vastness of the landscape and the rhythm of walking in tune with the camels and mules. As we waited around to get set up, we got chatting and he showed me some pictures from home. First of all his £6,000 mountain bike and then his six-month-old daughter Millie. He clearly loved both dearly. I liked his priorities.

I could see Zaid and his family over in the distance at their camp, but we had to wait to get everything organised for filming before I could go up. Finally, off I set with the drone buzzing overhead. A drone in flight makes a sound like a large, angry wasp which was pretty disconcerting. I had to concentrate hard not to keep looking up at it and focus on where I was going.

It was wonderful to see the family again. Zaid and his mother Aisha were unchanged but Zara had grown into a young woman, a carbon copy of her mother, Izza. Little Aisha had been a baby when I last saw her and now she was a toddler with attitude. Throughout the time we spent together, she would strike poses like a super model on the catwalk, whenever she spotted the camera. Baby Brahim was a new addition and quickly became a favourite with everyone. There was a lot of cooing.

Zaid's mother, Aisha, looks like she has been carved from granite. She is extremely striking, with deeply tanned and lined skin, a strong nose and thoughtful eyes. She is absolutely the matriarch of the family and Zaid consults her for every major decision. One of the things I had remembered about her was how warm she was, even in the cold, her hands were like little hot water bottles.

We had arrived late and as soon as the greetings were over, Zaid started to break camp. I tried to help with taking down the tent but felt that I was doing more harm than good so demoted myself to porter and ferried things between the camp and the pack animals. For this journey we had two adult camels and two babies, two mules, two donkeys and a baby donkey and around 250 goats. Then there was us and the drone crew. There was no problem with carrying equipment as one mule was designated as the camera mule and was loaded up with an array of tripods, batteries, chargers and sundry things in black boxes.

And we are off, marching across the plain. I walk at the back with Aisha and Zara. Aisha tells me she isn't feeling well and takes any chance she gets to sit down and rest. In front of us the animals plod on. The rhythm is entirely governed by the convoy of animals and we slow down and speed up with them. It is intensely calming as all autonomy is taken from you and you are just following. One small donkey was very heavily laden. Twice she fell over a boulder as she was going uphill and had to be hauled up to standing again by Zaid and the muleteers.

I was fascinated by the camels, especially by their feet. They walk very elegantly and precisely, and the soles of their feet puff up and down like hover crafts. No obstacle seems to faze them, they just glide over it, and keep going.

I'm brought out of my trance by a crackling noise coming from my pocket. Alicia has given me a walkie talkie as she knew we were going to get spread out. She needs us to stop. Séamas has been taking wide shots and now they need to catch up. I ask Zaid to stop. He isn't keen.

"Beaucoup du travail, beaucoup du travail," he says. He wants to get to camp so that he can sort out the animals and set up camp before dark. Also, his mother is sick and he doesn't want to keep her waiting on the road and he says the children are hungry. We have already delayed things with the drone shots.

We set off again. Zhhzhh goes my pocket and we stop again. This is repeated about half a dozen times over the next few kilometres. By this time, Zaid is actually angry. He is locked into his schedule by the needs of his animals and family and the short hours of daylight in November. Alicia and Séamas have to do their job and get the shots or we won't be able show the audience what the life is like. I am stuck in the middle and beginning to feel it.

"Beaucoup du travail, beaucoup du travail." and the "Zhh zhh" of the walkie talkie war with each other. I am being a bit of a coward now and hanging back behind Zaid to try and avoid some of his wrath but Alicia needs me to talk to him as we are walking. I gird my loins and approach. Apart from his frustration with the filming process, we have a language problem. Zaid speaks Tamazight, which is the Berber language from this region and I speak a bit of Tashlaheet, which is the Berber language from the High Atlas and entirely different. Zaid speaks some Arabic and a little French so we manage. But at this stage we are on a hiding to nothing. You have to want to communicate in order to communicate, and he really doesn't. I feel a bit baffled and upset as I had come into this imagining we would pick up where we left off last time, which was as friends. We struggle on for a bit and he tells me about how he came into the nomadic life but in the end, we give up and walk on in silence. I'm hoping its companionable.

The terrain changes to become more rocky and with narrower paths and we start to come down the last part of the route to where we are going to spend the night. It is a flattish bit of relatively clear ground, shielded by slopes and with a little stream running down. There is a rough stone enclosure in a bad state of repair where the goats can go. I admire Alicia enormously, she definitely has bigger balls than me. She wants to film us properly coming into camp so tries to get Zaid to stop. This effort has a Canute like inevitability to it. Not only is Zaid in no mood to turn back, but all the animals have spotted their camp and are an irresistible force. There is no way to stem this tide and we all move down into the valley.

Life on a caravan train appears to me to be long periods of Zen-like gentle movement followed by spurts of frenetic activity. When we get to camp, it is all hands on deck and we set to. We have to get the camp organised before it gets dark and the sun is sinking fast.

First of all the pack animals are unloaded and the two youngest kids are bundled up nice and warm in the shelter of the wall of the goat enclosure, with just the little pointed hoods of their jellabas sticking out. Then, we attend to the goats who have been brought up by Izza. The goats are held at bay, as before we let them into their shelter we need to rebuild it. It is a round pen made of large stones piled up on each other. Clearly, the animals partially destroy it every time they are here, or perhaps the weather does. The basic structure is there but there are rocks scattered everywhere. Everyone who doesn't have another job, starts piling them up again. I suffer a crushed big toe as I destroy a bit of wall I am trying to build and Séamas and Alicia court death by leaning on parts of the very dodgy construct, aiming to get the best shots.

Once the pen has been restored to palatial condition, the goats are herded in, to a cacophony of bleats. One poor soul though is kept aside.

Then we put the tent up and try to get it done quickly because it has started to rain a bit. Zaid has obviously decided that I am now one of his secondary wives or aunties and I am given a proper job to do. What a relief, I hate just hanging around or even worse, trying to look busy when I am not. My job is to sew up the tent over the posts. It is a goats' hair tent, made by Aisha, Zaid's mother, from wool gathered and spun from their own herd. It is held up by wooden poles, worn smooth by long use. I am handed an iron needle the length of my forefinger and the width of a kitchen match, with a thick twine threaded through. Izza shows me what to do, which is basically sewing the top of the tent to the sides using big, running stitches. Thank goodness for those sewing classes in primary school at St Denis' and Cranley's Academy for Young Ladies in Edinburgh. Then, it was a seersucker rose nightie. ho knew that I would be using the skills learnt on a nomadic tent in the Jebel Saghro? When it is up, the tent is about 7 metres by 4 metres, pretty big. You have to crouch down to get in, but can sit upright inside and stand almost upright in the middle. Because it is winter, three of the side flaps are secured down, but one is left half open for easy access to the cooking area. The floor is covered in rugs, with thin mattresses and woolly blankets to sit on. Of course, a pot of tea is already on the boil.

Next task is to collect water. Izza has taken pity on me and I am now firmly under her wing, which suits me just fine. She takes me off to the stream that we passed earlier. We have four big plastic carriers between us – the kind that hold car windscreen wash but much bigger. Izza uses the trip to teach me something. We first go to a pool down near the valley. It is about the size of a large wash basin and is still. She tells me that this is no good for us and pools some water in her hand to show me the minute green algae spores in it. She indicates that the animals can drink from it. We then turn upwards and climb much higher to a smaller pool that is filled with clear water and has a tiny waterfall flowing into it. We fill up the containers. She straps one to her back with her shawl and carries the other, and I grab my two, happy that at least I can do this. I am having no problems talking to her even though we don't share a language. When you are doing things together it doesn't matter.

As we get back to the camp I spot Zara coming down from the peaks opposite. She is almost invisible under a gigantic pile of kindling and wood scraps. All the food is cooked on wood that is gathered in situ. There are very few trees here and junipers are protected by law, so almost all the firewood is dried up scrubby herbs and bushes.

We are having a celebration tonight in honour of our presence, which means goat kebabs so it is time to collect and slaughter the lonely goat who has been kept aside. Of course, Alicia wants to film it and she wants me to watch it. Now, I will freely admit to being a hypocrite. I eat meat and I like it but I really don't want to acknowledge that it comes from a live animal that is dying so I can enjoy its flesh. I absolutely do not want to watch this goat being killed and I absolutely do not want to be filmed watching this goat being killed. However, the fact is that I have no choice, and I do understand why. We want to show all parts of what life was like and killing animals is a completely natural part of it. I still don't want to do it, though. I suppose at least I am not being asked actually to do the killing. For the record, I would have said no, because I would have botched it and caused the animal unnecessary pain.

Zaid and Ali take the goat firmly in their arms and move about 200 metres away from the camp up a rocky ravine. The goat is crying but doesn't appear to be in terrible distress. I am feeling very unhappy. Séamas asks me to tell the camera what we are doing.

"I am walking up a ravine to watch a goat being slaughtered," I say. "I don't want to do it at all but I am being forced to for TV."

"You sound really petulant and glib," says Séamas, "Try again." He is right and I do.

It's time. Ali holds the goat and Zaid slits its throat straight through the windpipe and the artery. It is immediately still and quiet but then spasms as the oxygen fails to get to the brain and the blood fails to get to its heart and it dies. The spirit is quickly gone.

It is actually a quick and decent death. I suspect it is infinitely kinder than our industrial methods where animals are transported in trucks away from their habitats, crowded together and then killed en masse. The fact is, that if I want to eat meat, I have to be aware of where it comes from and how it is killed.

Zaid is working away at the animal. He cuts a hole in the skin and then puffs at it. He basically blows it up like a balloon, it is the most extraordinary thing to see. This separates the skin from the flesh and makes it easier to remove. Once he has done that, he peels the skin completely off in virtually one go, turning it inside out. Then he starts to gut it and cut it up. I am released and head back down the hill. I want a quick break from everyone and everything.

My new mentor, Izza, hands me a cup of tea and shows me what she is doing. She is making the bread at the cooking area of the tent. It is basically flour, water, a little salt and a little bit of some kind of rising agent, we pound and pound and pound it in a basin and then knead like demons, if demons were to knead. After we are done, we leave it in the basin covered over by blankets and a rug so that it can rise. It is put beside the two littlest children who are covered up in blankets like cocoons waiting for their dinner. It is dark now and although the rain has stopped, it is bitterly cold. Later we shaped it into flat loaves, like nan and these were cooked on top of a rounded iron pot like a wok which was upside down over the fire.

I have been communicating well with Izza but I want to talk about more abstract things with Aisha so we get Omar, who works for Charlie and who will be cooking for the crew, to translate. He is a Tamazight speaker but also speaks French and Arabic so can communicate with all of us.

I asked Aisha what life was like for her, rather expecting her to say it was wonderful to live in this way. But she didn't. She told me that she was old now and this life in the mountains was too hard for her. She would prefer to stay down in a village. She said that everything was changing for them and that it used to be better before. There were more people living and herding in the mountains, more families, more goats. Now, the way of life was dying and it was getting harder. It was difficult to hear that, sitting as I was by a glowing campfire under the stars, surrounded by a family working in harmony, living a life that looked so good in so many ways from the outside.

The men were busy, meanwhile, making the brochettes. Offal is the most sought after part of the goat as it is considered to be the tastiest bit. The goat's heart, kidneys and liver were being chopped up for the kebabs. I had come to terms with the goat killing and felt fine about eating it. Pieces of each were skewered on and then covered in fat to make them tasty and help them cook. These were roasted over the open, and very smoky, fire beside the tent. The intestines were unravelled, squeezed out like tubes of toothpaste and cooked separately. As a Scot, I like my offal and was looking forward to my dinner, although I was concerned the tubes of intestine were a step too far.

Zaid had mellowed out and, with Omar to translate, we were able to have a chat. I wanted to understand the economics of herding and the nomadic life, how they survived. He told me that he had built up his flock to 210 goats – the sheep having died in the drought. Water is a constant pre-occupation for him, just as it would have been for the caravan trains. When it rains in Morocco, everyone is happy and says things like, "It is raining, Thanks be to God. Or Have you seen the rain? Good for the crops. A blessing." There had been a drought in the region and it had affected him badly. He had had to spend over €1000 on feed for some sheep he had in his flock, but he lost 35 of them through starvation. Goats eat anything, but sheep are fussier.

Zaid has bucks and ewes in his herd so they breed naturally. In terms of value, a good goat can get £110 at market, a medium one makes around £65 and at Eid time, a good goat can go up to £200. Eid means holiday or feast and during the big holiday after Ramadan which is called the Feast of the Sacrifice, every family who can afford it buys a goat or a sheep to slaughter. Even the supermarkets set up special livestock pens in the car park so you can go and get your Eid sheep.

There are markets in the various towns the nomads pass through and Zaid sells 3-5 goats at a good one. The money is then used for essentials like flour, tea, sugar, vegetables and anything else his family needs. He also uses the money to buy transport animals and sometimes hire them in. Then there are school expenses for Maymoun, although Maymoun lodges with Zaid's brother when he goes to school. Zaid's flock is his entire capital and also livelihood so it is easy to see why the first thing we did was make the animals secure before we even set up the tent.

My tummy is rumbling and I am really glad when the dinner and the goat skewers are ready. But we are about to hit another cultural hitch. Hospitality and generosity are a vital part of life for the nomads. The idea of sitting down to eat and not sharing everything is incomprehensible to them. Of course, for the film, Alicia and Séamas have got to be filming rather than eating. A struggle ensues. Zaid just cannot understand or accept that they have to film before they can eat and that they are not going to sit in the circle with us. Alicia explains that she is not being rude or refusing the food but just needs to film the segment of us eating first. It doesn't really wash. My tummy rumbles some more. We are saved from an international incident by Omar and his translation. The family and I eat, Séamas and Alicia film and then come and join us and peace is restored.

After supper, there is a bit of downtime and I show Izza and the children the pictures I took of them from two and a half years ago. They love them and my phone is passed round to everyone amongst gales of laughter. I try to talk to Zara but she has regressed to being really shy with me, although she obviously remembers the little sheep that she was holding up in one of the pictures.

I go out to brush my teeth and walk away from the lamplight of the tent. The stars are so bright that I can pick each of them out. The traveller's reward. I take a long time doing my teeth, enjoying the night, the solitude and the sounds of laughter and chat coming from the group.

The crew have all put up their little one man tents further down the valley, near to Omar's mess tent, but I get to sleep with the family. Zaid is kipping down outside the tent, he says to guard it but maybe he also wants a bit of peace and quiet. The rest of us are all in there together. Once again, I put on all my available clothes, including my bobble hat.

Zara helps me make my bed. There is a thin mattress on the floor of the tent. I lie down on it in my sleeping bag and then she puts a blanket and then a rug over me. She is next to me. Once I am in, I am very snug and comfy and warm and I like the feeling of sleeping all together under one goats' hair roof. I am full of meat and bread and tired after a full day of travelling and sleep comes quickly. 2.30 I wake up, freezing cold but not wanting to move because Zara is sound asleep beside me.

"Blanket hog!" I silently accuse her. I can hear the mules chomping outside and the dogs barking but inside the tent everyone is quiet. I try and wiggle into a bit more warmth without making any noise. I think warm thoughts and try the trick of imagining a hot spot in my chest and then mentally pushing it down my arms and legs into my fingers and toes. The mental effort works and I fall asleep again until 5.30 am when it is time to get up and I find that Zara had not stolen my blanket, it had just scrunched its way down to my feet.

I get up quickly to go and find a space to have a morning pee and admire the dawn. The sun hasn't risen yet so everything is semi-dark and silhouetted. I am walking back to the camp when one of the shepherd dogs blindsides me. It runs up and bites down on my leg. This is not good.

"You were coming up with the light behind you, so all it would have seen was a shadow, a stranger," said Séamas afterwards. I think he is right but rabies is a big problem here in Morocco and even though I have had the anti-rabies jabs after being bitten by a cat in the summer, if the skin is broken I will have to get to a doctor and get another course of the vaccine.

A trickle of blood rolls down into my sock. "Bugger," I think, "this is going to cause havoc with Laura's schedule." I sit down and pull up my jellaba, trousers and running tights to have a look. The skin is broken and a bit of blood is coming out but when I look at my trousers they aren't ripped, so the dog's teeth and saliva had never actually come into contact with my skin. What a relief. I just have a bruise and a bit of a cut. In fact, it took over three months for the cut to heal which was a bit weird but at least we kept on schedule.

73

Laura and Alicia spent breakfast gleefully concocting fantasy emails for Angela at Tern TV, who is in charge of Health and Safety.

"Alice has been bitten by potentially rabid dog in the middle of the Jebel Saghro, please advise."

Packing up the camp was much easier this time, and we were up and off quickly. There was one thing that illustrated how unsentimental you have to be to live this life. One of the dogs was missing, she was pregnant and Izza thought she had given birth in the night. She went off to find her. She came back with her tied to a rope. The puppies were either killed or just left behind as the family couldn't afford to keep them. All food is valuable. The dog howled for three hours.

Zaid had relaxed a lot. I think he had got used to us and the vagaries of television and he even joked when he heard the walkie talkie go off for the first time that morning.

"Arret, arret" he said with a big smile, "Zhh zhhh". This day's trek was along stony and rocky ground around the side of one of the mountains. We were splitting up from the crew as they wanted to go to the other side of the hill to get wide shots.

The next few hours were wonderful. Free of any need to stop and start, we could just go with the flow and walk as the family normally would. As our little caravan progressed, it was trampling on the ormilus plant which grows everywhere in that region. It smelt a bit like chamomile, and we were surrounded by a delicate scent. Zaid came back with a bag of squishy dates and I tucked in. The Kendal mint cake equivalent in Morocco.

Zara was laughing and running around, like the child she still is. At one point, she came up to me and slipped her hand into mine to walk with me for a while. Sharing is instinctual here. On the walk, I had lent my poles to Maymoun to try out. He loved them, he was so proud, walking in front like our guide, checking back to make sure we were all following and joyously prodding every piece of dung on the route. But when I looked up five minutes later, he had made one of the poles shorter and given it to his little brother, Hassan, so they could both enjoy it.

It is a small example of the core value of this culture. It is completely communal, everyone sleeps in the same place, eats from the same bowl of food, takes their share of the work and sits together in rest time. It would be very hard to be lonely.

We arrived at our destination and had a last meal together. All the difficulties of the past couple of days were forgotten in a pot of sweet, mint tea. As we kissed goodbye and left the family to the rest of their journey, I thought about what Zaid had told me about this life, which is so idyllic to dip into.

"It is very hard to carry on as nomads," he said. "Always moving. Always cold. Electricity, television are coming and everything is changing. The government is building roads everywhere. I want my younger children, Aisha and Hassan and Brahim, to go to school. Maybe we will settle down with a small farm so they can do that. I have no choice. Change is here."

This trek had given me a chance to experience a little bit of what it would have been like to travel with a caravan hundreds of years ago. Now, though, we were back on the hunt for clues from the trade routes.

Chapter Five

*"We arrived after 25 days at Taghaza. It is a village with no good in it.
Amongst its curiosities is the fact that the construction of its houses and its
mosques is of rock salt with camel skin roofing and there are no trees in it, the soil
is just sand. In it is a salt mine. It is dug out of the ground and is found there in
huge slabs, one on top of another as if it had been carved and put under the
ground. ...The blacks exchange the salt as money as one would exchange gold
and silver. They cut it up and trade with it in pieces. ...We stayed in it but ten
days in miserable condition, because its water is bitter and it is of all places the
most full of flies."*

Ibn Battuta, Al Rihla.

"Will you be safe?" asks Alicia.

"Yes of course I will,"

"Are you sure? You are happy to get in the truck or car on your own?
I don't want you to do it if you aren't."

I am touched by this concern for my personal welfare from Alicia
and briefly a scene from The Hitcher flashes through my mind and
freaks me out. But in fact, hitchhiking in Morocco is very common
and very safe. Granted there aren't that many single, western women
standing by the side of the road with their thumbs stuck out, but I am
confident that I am going to enjoy the experience.

The sun is starting to set and the dust motes are dancing a golden waltz over the long, straight road. A tourist bus looms and I holster the thumb, I don't want to end up paying for my ride. The next vehicle appears on the horizon and chugs towards me, and chugs and chugs and chugs.

About 50 metres before it gets to me, I hear the brakes being put on and it rattles to a slow halt. It is half Landrover, half jalopy, literally tied together with bits of string.

"Peace be upon you,"

"Upon you be peace,"

"Where are you going?"

"Sijilmassa."

"I'm going in that direction, get in, get in."

I clamber in, shake hands with my benefactor and go to shut the door. Brilliant! It shuts with a bolt which pushes across the frame and the door itself. The handle is long gone. Abd el Ghani, the driver, pushes the pedal to the metal and we shoot off at 10km an hour.

Abd el Ghani is a modern trader. He hunts fossils in the Saghro and then sells them to wholesalers and to tourists from his base in Erfud. That's his first job. His second is to provision the desert nomads in the area. I tell him that I have just been with Zaid and his family, who it turns out that he knows and we become firm friends. We arrive all too soon and I leave after promising that I will stop off for couscous with him and his wife the next time in Erfud. Apparently, she is a very good cook.

Sijilmassa. I have lived in Morocco for three years and I had never even heard of the place until now. It was a thriving city in the high years of the trans-Saharan trade and very important in its history. Fortunately, I was going to have an expert guide in Chloe Capel, an archaeologist working in the region, to help me discover the secrets of this lost city.

I set off to find the site, which was not that easy. No signs, no blue plaques, no interested sightseers. I had asked the way and knew I was on the right route but I appeared to be in the middle of a very large building site. I climbed a little hill and there, spread out, were the ruins of what had once been the greatest city in the whole of southern Morocco and the richest city on the trade route itself after Timbuktu. Ozymandias came forcibly to mind. Almost nothing was left, there was no tumbleweed but there should have been. This city was the Manchester of its day and now only a few crumbling walls remain. I was going to need Chloe to tell me the city's story and interpret the rubble.

Sijilmassa was founded in the late eighth century and it means "a place where there is water" in Berber. The city was built in the middle of the largest oasis in Morocco, the Tafilalt oasis which is famous for its dates, and from where I was standing I could see the date palms stretching out into the distance – stretching right over to the far hills where there is an old Almoravid fortress which was built to protect the trade routes and also to collect taxes from the travelling merchants.

Water is provided by the Ziz, which is not a river but a canal. The canal runs for 40km between Erfud and Merzouga and is the only structure of its kind in North Africa. It was the aorta of Sijilmassa, giving it the means to grow enough food to provision the traders. This much I knew but I was very excited to pick our archaeologist's brain, as she specialises in trans-Saharan trade and the mediaeval period. I was also dying to meet her as Charlie, Alicia and Laura, who had all met her before on a site near Marrakech in September, absolutely loved her. I had had weeks of listening to:

"Chloe's so lovely."

"Chloe's so gorgeous, and so cool."

"Chloe just knows so much about everything and she is so engaging."

"Chloe is so clever, I just learn so much from her."

Who was this paragon? More beautiful than Angelina Jolie, nicer than Jennifer Aniston, cleverer than Einstein, more inclusive than Nelson Mandela… I was sure she couldn't live up to the hype and of course I was prepared to hate her on sight.

She was waiting for me on a slope looking out over the main square of the site and came bouncing over to introduce herself, with big, clear eyes shining from under her little archaeologist's cap. Dammit. She did live up to the hype and was instantly likeable. She was so full of enthusiasm for the site that a pile of rubble transformed into a glimmering city in front of my eyes. Originally from Normandy, she told me that she wanted to become an archaeologist because her parents worked the land, "peasants", she said, and so she loved the outdoors and working with her hands but she was also good at school.

The first thing I wanted to know was about this unique canal and what that meant for the origins of the city.

"It appears that the system was created all at the same time," she told me. "It means that from the beginning, the oasis was as big as today. So it is clear that it was too much just for the inhabitants of Sijilmasa and that's why we can guess it was for many more people than themselves so that's why we think it's a kind of economic program from the beginning."
The city covers 14km from end to end, boundaried in the east by Bab Ria (the windy gate), although the oasis itself is much larger and measures nearly 50km. The main square housed the mosque, the madrassa and probably the barracks. Rich people lived on the slightly higher ground, whilst the poorer folk stayed lower down where there were also the markets and the storage areas.

The buildings themselves were made of mud blocks. The method of construction is still used today. Two wooden sheets are placed to form a gap, the mud is pushed in and then pressed down as hard as possible. It is left to dry and then oil or water is poured on top to make sure it is compressed enough. If the liquid soaks down, it isn't. If the liquid stays where it is, the next layer is added. The walls that are made this way are perfect for Morocco's climate because they retain the warmth in winter and the cool in summer. They have given way to concrete which is much faster and cheaper to build with, but does not regulate temperature in the same way and there is a movement, by those who can afford it, to going back to this traditional method.

The inhabitants of Sijilmassa must have been relatively rich and certainly enjoyed one of life's finer luxuries. Many of the houses that have been excavated have indoor toilets, something that is unheard of in this area for this period of time. Good news for the merchants arriving after so many days on the road, too.

Standing overlooking the main square, Chloe, brought it alive for me. The central building was the mosque and I could see the outlines on the ground of where the pillars would have been. They were built of brick and these had long been carried off by the townspeople to build houses. The place where the big, main door had been was still visible but when the door was taken, it caused the walls on either side to collapse. Chloe pointed out some holes in the compacted mud of the remaining walls. That was for a kind of internal scaffolding she told me, so that when the walls had to be maintained and rebuilt, they could slot in long beams of wood to do it. The same method is used in the great mosques of Timbuktu.

All around us in the sand, were little bits and pieces of glazed clay. At first sight, they were no different from the bits of stone that were scattered around but then Chloe picked up a flattish piece with a nobble on top and explained.

"You can see it is a bit of pottery because of the shape, because of the paste, because of the painting on the top. There are numerous clues to give the date of the ceramics and here it has been produced with a potter's wheel. It's actually a lid you could put on top of a cup or a little jar for water, for service on the table – maybe for people just to take water to lunch. I think it's probably 12th – 14th century." Suddenly, those little pieces of green/blue took on a whole new significance and we started shard hunting. Séamas had to work the camera but Alicia, Laura and I were down in the dust, searching for treasure. All you could hear echoing around the site was, "Found a bit. Found a bit." We kept queuing up with our handfuls of pieces to get Chloe's opinion. It was really exciting, and between the three of us we had accumulated quite a mound.

Suddenly, Séamas' voice broke into our collectors' frenzy. "I'm sure the BBC would be delighted to know you three are looting everything in sight," he observed, drily. Three guilty faces turned to him, and we reluctantly put our shards back on the ground where they belonged. With all this booty just lying around, I asked Chloe why it hadn't been explored more by archaeologists.

"There are two main reasons. The first one is about science. The archaeology here is quite difficult so there aren't so many researches on this site, because it's a huge site, very looted and complex, so archaeologists don't dare to work here! It's hard to find someone courageous enough to work there. But the main reason is because Sijilmassa became a kind of myth and you don't want to know many things about a myth. It's a myth because of gold, because of the fame of the city, because of its richness, because it was a green place in the middle of desert. And, it's the cradle of the dynasty who rules Morocco today. You don't want to be disappointed with the real history of the city."

In its glory days, Sijilmassa was the pivot in the gold trade between the ancient kingdom of Ghana and Europe across Morocco. It had a virtual monopoly on gold at this time. In the late 700s it was so confident in its economic strength that it declared independence from the Abbasid Caliphate which ruled the Islamic world from Baghdad.

There was a large local Jewish population who monopolized the minting of currency, and the coins minted in Sijilmassa were used all over Europe and have even been found as far away as China.

The traders came up from the south with their rough gold, rested and refreshed in Sijilmassa and turned their gold into coin, then either sold it on or continued up towards the northern hubs of Marrakech and Fez, from where the gold found its way to Europe. It was a massive service station for provisioning and stocking the caravans during their journey. From Sijilmassa the southern route to Timbuktu was Sijilmassa – Taghaza – Taudenni – Timbuktu. On the way back down the merchants would be carrying great slabs of salt as well as leather goods, ironwork and cloth.

As the trade routes shifted so did Sijilmassa's prosperity and as the routes dwindled in importance, so did the city. In the eighteenth century it had its last great flourish when Sultan Moulay Ismail rebuilt it, but in 1818, a thousand years of history came to an end when it was sacked and destroyed by the Ait Atta, the same tribe that Zaid and his nomad family are from, and the dominant nomadic tribe in the region.

It's sobering how absolutely a great city can disappear from the face of the earth. As I stood and looked at it now, it was hard to believe the stories that Chloe told of merchants from all over Africa and even Europe, of goldsmiths hammering away at gold coins, of thousands of camels drinking at the Ziz canal.

My mind was full of this and I started to compare the past with the present and our future. Is this a history lesson of what Brexit might mean for Britain? Will our trade routes effectively be gone and will we dwindle into nothingness? Will the equivalent of the Ait Atta, our bombastic world powers Trump and Putin, unleash Armageddon onto some of the world's great cities and leave them as ruins? These sombre thoughts, dominated my goodbye to the lovely Chloe, but were soon blown away as I faced an unexpected but nearly fatal experience.

I was heading off to the market in nearby Rissani and the easiest way to get there was by donkey cart. There were lots passing, so I flagged one down. Now, Health and Safety is a big deal for TV production companies and the BBC in particular. Before I came, I was asked many questions to cover all sorts of contingencies. Here is one of them texted to me by Laura.

"Alice, have you ever ridden a donkey???. Please say yes.... It's for a risk assessment."

"Yes, I have ridden many an ass in my time."

"☺"

We were covered. I happily got up onto my cart and said hello to my driver, Mohammed. He looked so nice and kind. I couldn't guess his exact age but it was definitely seventy plus (quite a lot plus) and I had to shout to be heard. Off we trotted and, as we started down the hill, it became apparent that Mohammed had no control whatsoever over his trusty steed and this steed was not so trusty. We gathered speed and headed for the rim of the hill which gave over to a steep drop. Séamas had attached a gopro camera to the cart so that they could record my expressions, no doubt expecting shots of me happily enjoying the experience. What they got was sheer terror and repressed shrieking. Alicia later told me that she and Bill the editor were weeping with laughter when they saw the footage in the edit suite. The donkey had picked up the pace and was now racing towards the brink, Mohammed's hands were completely slack on the reins, and I was wondering if I should bail and risk some nasty cuts and bruises. What was Mohammed doing? Had he lapsed into some kind of coma? His eyes were still open but it felt like no-one was at home.

"Mohammed, stop, stop, slow down, go on the road," I yelled as loudly as I could. He jerked out of his dream and between the two of us we pulled on the reins and steered the runaway donkey away from the precipice. That donkey had a death wish. All the way into Rissani, it pulled suicidal manoeuvres.

"Truck coming towards us? Excellent, I'll cross the road into its path."

"4x4 overtaking? Fantastic, I'll just veer into its side."

"Bicycle? Ooh let me try and collide with it."

"Oh, my uncle, oh Mohammed, why is this donkey so mad?" I asked.

"Ah," he said, nodding wisely or perhaps senilely, "It is not my donkey. I borrowed it and you know a donkey will only obey its owner. It won't obey anyone else."

A fascinating insight into donkey psychology.

By the time we got into Rissani, I was a nervous wreck and couldn't wait to get off. Mohammed pulled up at the local pay and display.

This is a huge, open square full of tethered donkeys and mules. You pay the attendant and then you can park your donkey while you go into the next door market and buy what you need. You even get a ticket.

Rissani is a flourishing market town which has taken over some of Sijilmassa's role in that it now provisions all the people of the region. It is the nearest town of any size to the great sand dunes of Erg Chebbi and there are three market days a week instead of the customary one. Sunday, Tuesday and Thursday.

Out of curiosity I googled Trip Advisor's Top Ten Things to do in Rissani.

The first thing was to get out of it and visit Erg Chebbi, which seemed a bit harsh. Visiting the markets came in second and Sijilmassa was down there in ninth place, after walking tours and a visit to a souvenir shop. After spending some time there I feel qualified to say that the best thing to do in Rissani is to visit the market. It is the best market I have been to in Morocco. It has a totally different atmosphere to the equivalents up north. You can feel that you are in Africa. It is very large with different areas selling different goods. One thing that immediately struck me was that the men were dressed in white jellabas, very similar to the robes of the men in Sudan.

We were here to meet Hafida, who was going to be my guide across the dunes. But first I wanted to have a look round. I skipped quickly past the open air livestock suq, I knew what was happening there, and moved into the covered market. Row upon row of pristine, gleaming fruit and vegetables grown locally were succeeded by whole stalls specialising in olives and preserved lemons. Then came the clothes market, branching off into the pottery stalls. I had to stop to buy some cups. They make them from a slightly porous clay and glaze them with black around the rims. I am not sure of the scientific reason for this, but the end result is that if you use them for water, it acts like a mini fridge and cools the water down and it also makes it taste slightly smoky, which helps to take away the chlorine taste of the tap water. Also, I am a big fan of Lapsang Souchong tea and the flavour isn't dissimilar.

I could hear the ironmongers' section, before I saw it, with hammers banging away on metal, and the hissing sound of blow torches. You could see that we were in a primarily agricultural area from what was being produced. If you go to the ironmongers suq in Marrakech, it is all candle holders and nice hooks to sell to tourists, here it was shoes for donkeys and mules, axe heads, picks and hoes and lots of different sized nails.

Round the next corner, I stopped in my tracks. A man dressed all in white was sitting on the ground with his goods spread out in front of him, talking to a female customer. She was buying salt from a big pile which dominated his little collection of spices. I couldn't quite believe it. Here was a merchant selling salt, salt that had almost certainly come from a mine just like the one I had visited. Up until that moment, I had felt a little bit like a detective, sniffing out clues as to what this trans-Saharan trade was like and how it must have felt to be in a caravan. I had handled a gold coin from the era, I had walked through the ruins of Sijilmassa and I had gone deep into the mountain to see a salt mine. But here, for the first time, it somehow became real. Salt in its raw form being sold just as it would have been centuries ago, along the same route that the merchants travelled centuries ago. An unbroken chain of history. I crouched down and explained to him that we were filming a documentary about the salt routes and showed him the salt flower that Zac had given me in the mine. He smiled but I suspect he just thought I was a bit mad.

We'd arranged to meet Hafida in the date section of the market so that we could buy some to take on our trip. Our timing was excellent as we had come just at the end of the date harvest which takes place in October and November in Taflilat.

The date area of the market was large with permanent stalls along the sides and then different merchants in the middle with their piles of dates. Trade looked like it was pretty brisk.

Dates are a staple food all over North Africa and the Middle East, the original super food in many ways. It is said you can exist on just seven dates per day. I love them and if I am doing any long, hard trek or bike or run, I always take dates with me. Forget your high tech, expensive energy gels, a couple of dates will do the trick, and they don't make you feel sick. Dates probably originated from lands around Iraq and the name in English comes from the Greek word dactylos which also means finger. In Arabic, unsurprisingly, there are dozens of words for date, all meaning slightly different things.

Two of my favourite ones are: barhi, which comes from the Arabic for a hot wind. These dates are soft and rich, nearly spherical with thick flesh; my other favourite name is deglet noor, noor means light in Arabic, and these dates are golden in the middle when you hold them up to the light.

Fossils of date palms have been found dating back 50 million years, and archaeologists have found evidence of dates being cultivated in eastern Arabia as far back as 6000 BC. The Ancient Egyptians used them to make date wine, a potent brew by all accounts.

The date palm has separate male and female plants. Only the female plants bear fruit and one male plant can pollinate up to 100 female plants. Pollination used to be done solely by the wind but now is done manually either by the farmers climbing up the palm to do it themselves, or through wind machines.

Dates ripen in four stages, which are known by their Arabic names kimri (unripe), khlal (full-size, crunchy), rutab (ripe, soft), tamr (ripe, sun-dried). It can be confusing when you go to buy dates because the generic word for them is different in different countries. In Morocco it is basically tamr, but you have to add in all the words for the different stages, and the different varieties. It is a minefield. Prices, also, vary tremendously according to the quality and type of date you are buying.

Date palms can take up to eight years after planting before they will bear fruit. Once they do though, they can produce 68 to 176 kilos of dates per harvest season. There is more than one harvest season and there is a lot of work involved in cultivating them. They grow in large bunches and in order to get the best dates, the farmer has to thin them and put bags over them to help force them and also protect them from the birds. It looks quite comical when you walk through a palm orchard where all the dates are bagged up.

They are excellent energy food, 100 g of dates gives you around 282 calories, although it does vary depending on the type of date. Of that 80% is sugar but they also contain large quantities of minerals and vitamins including a high level of potassium which is needed in the heat to avoid cramp.

The seeds can be ground up and used as animal feed and the leaves and fronds are used to make brooms, while the fibre is twisted into ropes.

If you are not yet convinced of the general magnificence of the date then you should know that they were used to nourish Jesus. In the

Quran, Allah instructs Maryām (the Virgin Mary) to eat dates when she gives birth to Isa (Jesus).

Dates are actually mentioned over 50 times in the bible and 20 times in the Quran. Also, they are traditionally one of the first things you eat when you break your fast in Ramadan. Dates and milk - if you have been fasting all day, they taste like ambrosia must and the combination really does quench your thirst and immediately stop your hunger so that you can then relax and eat your break-fast normally.

As we were setting off to cross the Erg Chebbi dunes the following day, we needed to stock up on some of these little, squishy marvels, and Hafida was there waiting for us in the middle of piles of them. We chose a box of a yellow, quite crunchy variety and left to start our desert odyssey.

Chapter Six

"What makes the desert beautiful is that somewhere it hides a well."

Antoine de Saint-Exupéry, Le Petit Prince

Our desert odyssey starts tomorrow but first we have a night on the edge of the dunes. We're being driven there by the ever-cheerful Khalid. He has a wild head of hair, an encyclopaedic knowledge of everything we see en route, and strong Amazigh nationalist sensibilities. He and Séamas, with their revolutionary ideals, bond immediately and a week or so after the shoot in Morocco had finished, we had this text exchange.

"I hope you are well, my friend?"

"Hello Khalid, from all of us. I am here with Séamas and Alicia still in Mali. We are great. Timbuktu was amazing. I hope all is well with you."

"Did you finish the movie? All was good and safe? Say hi to Alicia plz."

"Yes. Everything is great and Alicia says a big hello back to you."

"Say hello to the lovely camera man plz. I love him."

The road is long and flat and straight with desert scrub on either side, punctuated with acacia trees. These produce a gum, if you cut the bark, which is slightly sweet and is believed to have many medicinal properties. It is called Gum Arabic and nowadays is used by the food industry as a stabiliser – it is one of the dreaded E numbers. It is, in fact, a type of edible glue. In Morocco, it is used like gelatine, or just to sweeten tea. Odder places that you find it are in shoe polish and water colour paints. The acacia tree for me, though, symbolises Africa. That distinctive silhouette, with its gnarled branches and flat top, etched against a big sky, is the memory of my childhood.

There is another shrub all along the route that I don't recognise but Khalid had the answer. It's the Apple of Sodom, the calotropis procera. It is about a metre tall with fleshy leaves and green globes. These are hollow and disappear in a kind of puff if you touch them but the flesh of the plant contains a milky, toxic sap which tastes horribly bitter and also sticks to you and won't come off even with soap. It's hard to pin down the origin of the name but I like Milton's reference in Paradise Lost. There he describes it as the fruit that Satan and his cohorts eat after having successfully tempted Adam and Eve to eat an apple from the tree of the knowledge of good and evil.

The next morning, I got up super-early to go for a quick run on the dunes. I was completely on my own just before sunrise in the dawn light. This was close to where Charlie and I had run when we competed in the Marathon des Sables in 2014.

The Marathon des Sables is a 156 mile ultra marathon across the Sahara. It is called the toughest footrace on earth and it almost broke

James Cracknell when he did it. It is around six marathons in six days, with the middle one a double, so you cover eighty kilometres in one go. You have to carry all your own kit and food for the week and the organisers provide communal tents for the night, and water. The temperatures during the middle of the day reach 50 degrees and your feet are pretty well guaranteed to be bloody stumps of pus by the end of it. Charlie had persuaded me that I could do it, after I finished riding the Tour D'Afrique, which was an 8000 mile bike race across Africa from Cairo to Cape Town and the subject of my first book, Dodging Elephants. We had trained together and talked of virtually nothing else for nine months, and it was the reason I moved to Morocco – to train in the exact environment. I am a truly terrible runner and wanted to give myself the best chance. For the record, we both finished. Charlie did brilliantly and was a speedster. He also looked ridiculously fresh every morning, as though he was about to step out for a quick game of tennis. I was very proud to come 665 out of 1100 runners. That moment of crossing the finish line is one of the highest points of my life and I cannot think of it without experiencing a rush of joy.

Our poor colleagues, though, were sick to the back teeth of it. There was mass flinching and some gritting of teeth every time a sentence started,

"When we did the Marathon des Sables….."

It was great to be back and this time I was travelling by camel across the sand towards Algeria, tracing the old salt roads. Hafida and I went out to meet our mounts and our camel driver, Ben Didi.

My experiences with camels to that point had been mixed. I have ridden them a couple of times and had fun but never achieved any kind of proficiency. When I was doing a taster tape for the series, I had taken one out in the Agafay desert and then talked to camera while holding on to its head so that we could both be in shot. It was no fool that camel and took advantage of my concentration to bite me hard. I think "wary" would be the word that described my approach as Hafida and I got to our little caravan.

Ben Didi helped us choose our animals. Hafida wanted the pretty white one and I wanted the gentlest one. He was a soft, dun colour with long eyelashes and seemed biddable. I called him Hamoun.

Safinat al Sahra – the ship of the desert. "Designed by God with the desert in mind,". Jamal, the generic word for camel in Arabic, comes from the same root as the word for beautiful, jameel. It's easy to see how it became camel in English, especially when you factor in that in countries like Egypt a 'j' is pronounced 'g' – gamal – camel. There are reputedly over a 1000 words for a camel in Arabic. I can't attest to that, but I am sure that I remember coming across one that meant," the young camel with blue eyes", when I was studying pre- Islamic poetry at Edinburgh University, but then I seem to remember a line that went, "He held his seething rope before him." Whatever the truth of the exact number, there certainly are a lot of them and they are very specific and often to do with water.

Al Ghab - a camel who drinks once every two days

Al Rabea - a camel who drinks once every three days

Melwa - a camel who is always thirsty

Al Riffa - a camel who drinks water whenever it can

Al Gasreed - a camel who does not drink much water

Caravans of camels are still used to transport goods. If you have ever driven through the Sudan, you will come across camel skeletons all along the route, which have died where they dropped. Some still have fur on, so are relatively recent.

In the great days of the trade, the caravans could be as big as 1000 camels, as merchants liked to travel together for safety. A fully-loaded camel could carry up to 200 kg and average 35 km a day. The pace is a steady four to five kilometres per hour which may not sound fast but factor into that the extreme heat and also a lot of climbing. Rolling dunes make for exhausting walking. The merchants would walk alongside their animals for long periods of time, to spare them and the camels would be strung out in single, or sometimes double, file with cords holding them to each other strung from tail to nose, secured to a brass ring.

Camels have a number of physical features which make them ideal for desert conditions. Their feet are designed for sand as the two toes and thick pads stop them sinking in. They have a good sense of smell when it comes to water and they can survive without drinking for up to ten days. This is not because they store the water in their hump, that is just fat as I saw in Fes, but because they can withstand very high temperatures and regulate their sweat so they don't dehydrate so quickly. Don't try kissing a camel because their lips are rubbery enough to munch on the thorny little plants that are scattered across the desert. And those lovely, long eyelashes serve a purpose other than vanity, they seal the eye completely when it is shut so that the animal does not suffer during sandstorms.

From Sijilmassa, there were two main trade routes across the Sahara. The first was slightly to the west, through Tawdenni in Mali and the second was more to the east through Tamentit in Algeria and then Tadmakkat and Gao in Mali and back west to Timbumktu. When the camels were plying their trade across the Sahara, the routes were long, difficult and dangerous. In essence, they still are.

One of the great difficulties for us was to be finding a route that would stay true to the original. Today, the border between Algeria and Morocco is a closed one. The only way to get across that border is to get special permission from both countries and in Morocco that means special permission from the king. If we wanted to take the route to Tamentit, we would have to get into Algeria, and the only way to do that would be to go all the way back up to Spain and then take the ferry from Almeria and come into Algeria that way. This would make a nonsense of us trying to follow the trade routes.

The other factor was the security risks in Algeria, which are very high. This is what the current foreign office advice on travelling to Algeria says:

"The Foreign and Commonwealth Office (FCO) advise against all travel to areas within:

- 450km of the Mali and Niger borders, with the exception of Tindouf town and Tamanrasset city
- 100km of the Mauritania border
- 100km of the Libya and Tunisia borders south of the town of Souk Ahras, with the exception of In Amenas

There is a high threat from terrorism in Algeria. Attacks could be indiscriminate, including in places frequented by foreigners. You should take great care at all times.

The main terrorist threat is from Al Qaeda in the Islamic Maghreb (AQ-M) and other regional Islamist groups including Al Murabitun and Daesh-affiliated Jund al-Khalifa. These groups pose a threat across Algeria, and have been active across the south, central and north eastern areas of the country and border areas of Algeria, Mali and Libya.

Kidnap

There is a high threat of kidnap against Westerners, particularly in the areas where the FCO advise against all or all but essential travel. Terrorists groups have kidnapped Westerners, Algerian government officials and civilians in Algeria and the wider Sahel region for financial gain and for political leverage. Further kidnaps are likely.

The long-standing policy of the British government is to not make substantive concessions to hostage-takers. The British government considers that paying ransoms and releasing prisoners increases the risks of further hostage-taking. This is also the position of the Algerian Government."

If you look at the map, the whole border between Algeria, Mali, Mauritania and Niger is coloured red. It was absolutely evident that this route would be impossible. It would be an act of unmitigated folly for a camera crew to set off by camel into an area where there is a high risk of kidnap. We would present irresistibly rich pickings to any terrorist group or indeed anyone that would like to capture us and sell us on.

We wanted to follow the route as far as we could though, so we saddled up, mounted up and set course for the Algerian border straight across the dunes.

I don't really understand what makes the desert so beautiful. It is just a big expanse of sand. There is something about it, though, that grabs your heart and won't let go. It was cold but the sun was bright and the sand gleamed all different colours of gold from platinum to rose. The dunes curved ahead and there was not another soul in sight. Our footprints on the sand were the first. Everything was sharp and pure. I could see individual grains of sand and tiny beetles crawling along. There were fox prints too. We didn't go in a dead straight line as I had expected. Ben Didi explained that some of the dunes were too steep for the camels, especially on the rim where they come to a very narrow edge and then plummet down.

We meandered along in total stillness and silence broken only by our occasional chatter. I rocked back and forward and let my mind drift. The camel behind Hamoun was very sociable and came right up beside us, resting his head on my leg so I could scratch his poll. It was so soft and curly. I scratched away and ignored the drool on my leg. I was starting to like camels.

Then the camel in front of me let out a roar and a transparent bubble of skin about the size of a small balloon lolled out of his mouth. Not an attractive look for anyone. I asked Ben Didi what it was and he explained that it was a sex thing. I felt that it wouldn't improve anyone's chances of sex, even a camel's. Apparently, I had got the wrong end of the stick. It was mating season and the camel was feeling frisky. No females were allowed in the caravan as they would drive the males mad with desire, so the bladder coming out of his mouth helped cool him down.

We had come to the base of a particularly large dune and Hafida said we should dismount and climb up it as this was a good spot to look over the coming terrain. We got off and shook out our legs. My bum had taken a bit of a beating so I was glad for a break. We waited for the crew to catch up. While we had been travelling on camel, they had been on foot as they needed enough distance from us to get wide shots. I couldn't help but feel that I had the best part of the deal. The dunes were hard to get up and over, and even more so when you are carrying camera kit. Calories were being burned apace and Alicia and Laura were glowing when they emerged out of the sands.

Hafida and I clambered to the top. There is definitely a technique to getting up and down dunes. You have to keep enough momentum to make sure you are constantly moving up and not just sliding back in the sand in a kind of treadmill effect. This is easy on the lower parts, where the gradient is easy, but increases in difficulty the closer you get to the top. I grabbed Hafida's hand and she pulled me up to the crest. From there, we could see straight across the dozens of kilometres that separated us from the Algerian border which was marked out by a low ridge of hills. I asked if she thought it would be possible to sneak across and got a firm no in reply. The border really was closed to us. Like kids we ran back down, sliding and slithering at great speed.

That night, Hafida, Ben Didi and I camped out under the stars. We found a sheltered spot in the lee of some low dunes and set ourselves up. The camels were hobbled and fed but wandered off to snack on the unappetising, thorny shrubs that grew in patches. I asked Ben Didi what their favourite treat food was, like sugar lumps for ponies. I should have known really, dates. Hafida and I broke open the box of yellow dates we had bought in Rissani and found our mounts. Hamoun was ecstatic. His rubbery lips snaffled up the dates from my hand and his eyes rolled in pleasure. Very soon, the box was gone but he followed me back to my bedding just in case.

We had laid out our stuff in a small semi-circle and built a fire in the middle of it. We had rugs to sleep on and put over us as well as our sleeping bags and bobble hats, and we needed them because not only was it very cold but it had started to spit with rain. There was no wind, though, as we were in the hollow. Ben Didi got the fire going, we put the tea on to boil and I settled down to hear Hafida's story.

Hafida is an extraordinary woman. She is the first female guide in Morocco and competes daily in a totally male environment. She supports her daughter and her mother, who are based in Marrakech, and takes out groups into the mountains and the desert. Morocco is a muslim country and that governs the behaviour that is expected of women. However, women's rights are written into the constitution, women work freely, many women do not wear a headscarf, women ride their motorbikes and bicycles in the streets, girls have equal rights to go to school and I only have to walk outside my front door, which is opposite the Faculty of Science in Marrakech, to see groups of young women going about their lives much as they would do in Edinburgh. However, it is still highly unusual for a woman to do the kind of work that Hafida does, which involves her being on her own with groups of men and also staying away from home on her own. Not only that, but the training is extremely difficult, based as it is on the French guide system. Legitimate guides in Morocco have to be certified.

In order to succeed with so many obstacles against her, I knew she had to be a very strong character and as she told me her story by the fire that night, I got to see what had forged her.

This is what she told me (slightly paraphrased as she was speaking in English which is her fourth language).

"My family were nomads from the south of Morocco from a little tribe to the south of Agadir. My great grandfather was a big warrior so he won a lot of battles and he became the chief of another tribe from the same area. He became a great man. My great grandmother was Ethiopian. She was a gift to my great grandfather because he had won the war.

"She was a slave but she was very beautiful. They gave her as a name, Shwanda, which means beautiful in our language and he married her.

When he married her, she became a free woman. She gave him a baby boy, so she was a very important woman. But my great grandfather had enemies from the new tribe and they killed him. They killed him and my great grandmother was left alone with the baby. He was about eight years old and they were very scared to stay there so she left to go back home and she left him. We don't know where she went– if she went back or if she became a slave to another family, we don't know.

"My grandfather, he just crossed all of Morocco, being bought and sold by different families. We were told that he was very brave and proud. Finally, he was bought by a family from near Marrakech in Tahanaout and this family was very kind to him.

"He was very proud because he did not think of himself as a slave since his father was a chief, but he couldn't marry a Berber white woman or an Arab so, he married another woman who was also a slave. She was called Kabira. That means a big woman because she was very tough and very strong and a good worker. He married her because she was black like him.

"She became pregnant with my father, but grandfather was angry about his history so he ran away from his family and went to the North. He left my grandmother and father who had not yet been born and he married a white woman.

"My father grew up a black slave. I guess you are surprised, but there was still a kind of slavery at this time. There were no named slaves but there were people who helped rich families. So, he was very poor and when he grew up, the French came and took him to be in the military and he served in Cambodia and Nigeria and was injured twice in the head.

"He married my Mum when he was 30 and she was just 11. She had her first baby at 12. We are five daughters. He was sick and drinking a lot and smoking a lot and he didn't work and we didn't have any food. My grandmother went to a French woman, Mama Regine, and she helped the family and my Mum brought us up.

"I can see that my family suffered but for me, now, I feel I am proud of this history and I know that it's great to be mixed from Berber, Ethiopian, African and Saharan women. I think that has given me courage. I don't think that things happen just like that. There is always something, pushing people to do things. I think doing my job, mountain guide, and desert guide, comes from that. I am the first female guide doing this job because it was just a job for men, for Berber men, and I found myself in 1994, the first woman who succeeded in doing it.

"My Mum says to me, "you are still a Nomad in your mind. And you really look like your great grandmother from Ethiopia." And I feel very proud.

"We don't really speak about slaves in Morocco, it's a bit taboo. Because it's a history of suffering. But it happened, it existed before the English people, for example, took slaves to America. It wasn't very long ago, just the 20th century. But now, I'm not thinking about this history as taboo or suffering, I'm thinking that my history gave me a lot of power and I am proud of it.

"And to all the slaves in the world, and in Morocco, we don't need always to say "okay this is a part of our life that broke us or made us less than others", no, we must know how to take this horrible thing and make it good.

"Maybe my grandma or my great grandmother or my great grandfather suffered a lot. But if they saw me now, they would be happy. They'd say okay, our line is thriving.

"This country is a mosaic. We have black, we have white, we have Arab, we have Berber, we have Jewish. We have a lot of faces, a lot of traditions, a lot of culture, and that makes this country really rich. That's why I'm very proud of our country."

As she told her story, Ben Didi put more wood on the fire so that it flared up highlighting Hafida's face. Her face that told the same story that she was telling, a beautiful, high-boned, almond-eyed Ethiopian face. What a story and what a woman.

The stars had come out and the light rain had stopped so we could see them clearly. Ben Didi had made another pot of tea while we were talking and now it was time for some music. He had brought along a little drum and started drumming and singing. Hafida and I joined in with a bit of clapping and humming and Hamoun snorted somewhere in the distance.

Then it was my turn and I whipped out my party trick. British reserve is of no use whatsoever around a campfire but fortunately years of being forced to recite poems or sing at ceilidhs has steeled me to all embarrassments. In fact, I like having a singsong or a dance and have long got over any feelings of shame. My party trick is Flower of Scotland in Arabic. First of all, I give a very colourful account of the history, which wins me many friends, then I explain that Scotland is a land of mountains and lochs where the men wear kilts and our tribes are known by their tartans. Lastly, I confirm that "Braveheart" is indeed a true account of our land and then off I go. "Ya ward iskotlanda…." It has not failed me yet.

I slept deeply and woke up to the clear light of dawn and a camera in my face. "Work away," said Séamas, "Work away." He and Alicia had snuck up over the dunes from where they had been camped to start the day nice and early.

Striking camp was easy as we were only carrying food, sleeping gear and the camera equipment. I wondered why Séamas hadn't done any filming from an actual camel, ie when he was riding it. He explained that the camels moved too much and the motion meant you couldn't get the right kind of shots.

But as we headed off across the desert again, it was everyone's chance to join the camel train so that we could be a proper caravan for a bit and forget the filming. Séamas, Alicia and Laura mounted up and for the next few hours the only cameras were on our mobile phones and we had a blast.

Chapter Seven

"After 25 days we reached Taghaza. It is a village with no attractions. A strange thing about it is that its houses and mosque are built of salt and roofed with camel skins. There are no trees, only sand in which is a salt mine. They dig the ground and thick slabs are found in it, lying on each other as if they had been cut and stacked under the ground. A camel carries two slabs. The only people living there are the slaves of the Massufah who dig for the salt. The Blacks come from their country to Taghaza and take away the salt. A load of it is sold at Iwalatan for 8-10 mithqals and in the city of Malli for 20-30, sometimes 40, mithqals. The Blacks trade with salt as others trade with gold and silver. They cut it into pieces and buy and sell with these. For all its squalor, quintars and quintars of gold dust are traded in Taghaza."

Ibn Battuta, Al Rihla

Our first route is blocked by the closed border with Algeria and the heavily-policed no man's land. There is no way to take the eastern road. We now have to head west and try the western path. A positive outcome from this is that it will take us past the great library of Tamegroute, a secret treasury of books and manuscripts.

As we saw in Fez, the trans-Saharan trade was not just about the trading of goods, it was also about the trading of knowledge and the spread of learning. Books and manuscripts travelled up and down the route as freely as the salt, gold and slaves that we had already found evidence of.

It is a long journey to Tamegroute and we have to go through Zagora where there is the famous sign post. It is a rusty old tin thing that points straight into the desert. Written on it are the immortal words "52 days to Timbuktu". We stop for lunch at a café that Charlie knows and tuck in to chicken and chips, lentils, olives, harissa, which is a hot chilli sauce that Séamas, in particular, is addicted to, and fresh fruit juice. It's a typical Moroccan roadside café lunch: fresh, simple and delicious. As usual, we are immediately surrounded by cats and they get fat as we pass them juicy chicken morsels.

Our conversation is standard for our lunches too. We cover a wide range of topics. First up, who wrote the score for Lawrence of Arabia? The answer is Maurice Jarre, Jean Michel Jarre's father. He also did Dr Zhivago, Dead Poet's Society, Ghost… I start humming the theme for Lawrence, much to the joy of the team. Then we move on to the word "twilight". Séamas claims it means the light before dusk and dawn. That is the first time I have ever heard that it relates to dawn too and I am inclined to pooh-pooh the idea, but he is right. I spend some time catching up on my journal.

"Anyone said anything witty, today?" I ask.

"I am constantly full of wit," parries Laura.

We move on to the lyrics of Hazel O'Connor.

"It's like you are speaking Chinese," says Laura, who is a good 25 years younger than the rest of us, "No cultural references whatsoever!"

It's time to get back on the road and I have to change out of road clothes to my tunic. I'm breaking out my special fancy purple one as we are going to meet a VIP.

"Make yourself look good," says Charlie, "this is the big one."

Tamegroute is a fairly non-descript place, but as we walk through the square by the mosque I spot the sign above the door to the madrassa and library. It uses the word "khazana". Khazana means treasure in Arabic and I immediately get excited. This is a treasury of books, hidden away in this town. Exploration commences.

We are met at the door by Haj Khalifa el Fasi and his son, Rachid. The Haj is very old and in a wheelchair. He is also very deaf. He has been the curator here since 1956, that is sixty years of service to preserving the intellectual history of the Maghreb. I hope that we can communicate well enough for me to truly benefit from the immense knowledge he holds. He has a real twinkle in his eye and goes in for a kiss on greeting.

"I reckon he had a twinkle in his eye every time he saw a woman," says Charlie later.

His family have been curators of the library in an unbroken line since the 1640s with the baton being passed from father to son. His forefathers would have been in this library during the days when the caravans passed, carrying books between Timbuktu, Marrakech and Fes. I'm struck again by how often history and the present are a continuum in Morocco.

Tamegroute is a Zawiya, an Islamic centre of learning, and has been so since the 11th century. It reached prominence five centuries later under the tutelage of Abu Hafs Umar bin Ahmed Al Ansari. Al Ansar means "the companions", the equivalent of the disciples in Christianity, and the name is used only to denote someone who is descended from one of the Companions of the Prophet, Mohammed.

In the 1600s it became the seat of the Sufi brotherhood of the Nasiriyya, founded by Sidi Mohammed bin Nasir al-Drawi. Sufism is the mystical branch of Islam which is also popular in Mali. Sufism isn't a sect as it crosses both Sunnism and Shi'ism, and Sufis claim they have existed since the first days of Islam. It is a polar opposite to the Islam of the Wahhabis and Salafites which inspires Al Qaeda and Daesh (Isis). The aim of Sufis is to obtain a direct connection with God.

Sufis of the Nasiriyya brotherhood carry out various ascetic practices, as well as a thorough observance of all traditional Islamic duties. Other Sufi schools can vary widely in their approach - for instance the whirling dervishes in Turkey are Sufis of the Mevlevi order - but the aim of all is the same: attaining a direct personal experience of God.

Sufism has many saints, which is a divergence from mainstream Sunnism and Tamegroute is still a place of pilgrimage as a result. The sick come to be healed by the Saint Sidi Mohammed bin Nasir al-Drawi. He is meant to be particularly good at curing anxiety and high blood pressure.

The buildings that we are in now are of a much later date. The Zawiya was destroyed by a fire but rebuilt in 1869 when the distinctive green, ceramic tiles of the area were used. Today, the Zawiya includes a madrassa, a shrine to Saint Sidi Mohammed bin Nasir al-Drawi, the library itself and a pottery which makes the green tiles. On the opposite side of the square, there is the mosque.

Malian students and teachers have come to study and to work here all through its existence. In the 17th century it is recorded that 1400 of them made the journey. We are told there are still descendants of those Malians, who came and never left, living in the town. It was also a stopping-off point on the pilgrimage to Mecca, because of the shrine of the saint.

Rachid wheels his uncle, The Haj, into the library and I follow. We go into a modern, light room with high ceilings that is lined with glass cases. It is tiled and there is a big conference table in the middle. It is so big and open that my voice echoes and booms out. We start the interview. The Haj, Rachid and I at the table and Séamas, Alicia, Laura, Charlie, and a couple of library workers working or watching from the other side. I am having to semi-shout my questions and begin to feel self-conscious. I am also having to concentrate extremely hard to understand the answers and I am nodding like a nodding dog sitting on a car dashboard with the effort.

"Alice, you are going to have to stop nodding like that. It looks like you are saying "oh you are really old so I am nodding hard to encourage you"," says Alicia.

She is spot on. I can feel myself going red with the effort and with the embarrassment of the whole situation: the shouting, the audience, the mutual lack of full comprehension.

I'm asking one question and getting a different answer back.

Alice: "A second question, the traders were not dealing only with leather, salt and gold, there was as well a book trade?"

Haj Khalifa (misunderstood the question): "There is not humidity here. Here the books are well conserved (preserved). The weather (air) is appropriate (for the conservation), and is not like in Dar el-Beida (Casablanca) or Rabat where there is humidity."

I have to stop periodically to translate for Alicia and I tell her that she really will need to get this one transcribed and translated as I am a bit lost in places.

However, there is no shortage of good will on all sides. We persevere and, with the help of Rachid, I get the information I need.

The Haj tells me that there are around 4,000 books currently in the library. There used to be up to 50,000 but over time they have been lost or gone to other libraries in Morocco and abroad. 2,500 of them are now in the national library in Rabat. The oldest book he has is a Quran which dates back to 1063. "That is three years before the Battle of Hastings" is the thought that flashes into my mind. He has also got one of Ibn Battuta's journals. I mentally plan to come back and persuade him to let me study it one day. Other things that catch my fancy are a collection of ancient Berber poetry written in Arabic script and a 15th century book of astronomy from Egypt that is illustrated with the signs of the zodiac, the planets and our solar system.

I want to focus on the links with Timbuktu, though, and see what clues he can provide to the trade in learning and knowledge. Al Haj doesn't disappoint. He tells Rachid to go to the case and take out one of the books. It is a book on Islamic jurisprudence by a scholar called Ahmed Baba el Timbukti. My ears prick up at the last name.

Ahmed Baba (1556 – 1627) is called Timbuktu's greatest scholar. He was a jurist from a long line of jurists and an expert in Islamic law and culture. He lived and wrote in Timbuktu but when it was conquered by the sultan of Morocco, he was accused of refusing to recognise his new lord's authority and of planning a rebellion. A warrior scholar. He was deported to Marrakech but was actually treated as an intellectual star there. He continued to teach and to practise law. He compiled a dictionary of Maliki jurists. Maliki is the school of Islamic Law that is practised in Morocco and Mali, which is still considered an important work today. He also continued to issue fatwas – religious rulings – which were praised for their clarity and adherence to Islamic law. When the sultan of Morocco died, Ahmed Baba was allowed to go back to Timbuktu where he kept on writing and wrote an Arabic grammar that is still used as the main Arabic textbook in northern Nigeria.

The book that was open on the table was an original book on jurisprudence, written by Ahmed Baba. This book is over 400 years old and it is solid evidence of that knowledge exchange that took place up and down this route. I am trying not to caper about with nerdy excitement but my voice goes up a few notches and squawks round the echoey room. Rachid takes me through it and I'm captivated.

It is a Q and A on various points of Islamic Law which admittedly does not sound as riveting as the latest John Le Carre but being this close to such a tangible piece of history and being able to read it in Arabic is thrilling to me. The calligraphy is quite simple so I can make it out. The absolutely best thing is that in the margins, there are written notes made by students all those centuries ago. I love the thought of my fellow sufferers in Arabic texts puzzling their way through the finer points. I know exactly how they felt and feel connected to them in spite of the years and cultures that separate us.

It is time to say goodbye to the Haj. I get a couple of kisses and an invitation to visit again but it is Alicia who is clearly the apple of his eye. There is a serious amount of flirtation going on that neither deafness, language, nor age is going to get in the way of. We virtually have to pry her hand out of his.

I have to do a quick piece to camera as we leave. This is where team work comes in. I am still flustered from doing the interview and my head is whirling. I rehearse what to say with Alicia and Laura, then I start walking and Séamas walks backwards and films. Disaster. I nearly knock the poor man into the flower bed. My coaches come to the rescue. Alicia gives me her best encouraging words and face, Laura gives me tips for walking more slowly and Charlie diplomatically exits the scene. We try again several times. Then, we get one, or so I think. Cue the immortal words from Séamas, "Now you've one in the bag, let's just go again." It's his mantra. We go. I get it. Bingo. High fives all round and we have the answer to the question, "How many people does it take to do a piece to camera?" The answer is four.

We are in desert country now, scatted with oases. The landscape is wide, flat plains with mountains fringing them and big, big skies. It is almost all sand and rocks with scattered acacia trees and thorny shrubs. I find it intensely relaxing, maybe because it is so spare and open. There are almost no people around, a very occasional shepherd with their flock, but that is it. Off the road, we sometimes catch glimpses of bright green, the small oases that indicate water, palm trees sticking their distinctive heads up into the sky. I spot a house in the distance, and fantasise to Charlie about buying it and becoming a hermit. He reckons I am just suffering a backlash from being with people 24/7 and having to be constantly outgoing with contributors but enters into the spirit with vigour, and points out every tiny hut and tent along the route.

"Look, Alice, there's a nice rock. You could set up camp there. A tarpaulin and a sleeping bag, you'd be all set."

We are heading towards the west now, and spend the night in Tighmert, an oasis on the way to Guelmim. It is so pretty and bursting with life after the empty spaces of the desert. The birds are singing full throttle and as we drive up a friendly dog comes to meet us and capers around, delighted at the company. It is like a garden of Eden. Date palms, vegetable patches, alfalfa, grain… every bit of ground is being used to grow things. The houses are made of compacted mud and are low and long. They are reddish brown against the green with brightly painted and patterned wooden doors. That night the moon positions itself just behind a palm and frames itself in the leaves and the sky is dark blue velvet.

Guelmim is our next stopping off point and I am getting there with a charming, long-haired French Anthropolgist called Romain Simenel who has spent a lot of time working in this region and is an expert in the trade and the people who ran it.

We meet up at a café and this is one of those moments where TV and life clash. He is with his Moroccan colleague, who I will call Rachid, as they are off to a meeting afterwards. For the film, we don't want his colleague to travel in the car with Romain and me, because it means extra on-camera introductions and possible confusion for the viewer. Alicia explains this very nicely to Rachid in French and offers him the front seat of the crew car. He is not having any of it and refuses. Alicia asks me to go over and explain again in Arabic and see if I can persuade him. I assume my friendliest manner, my best smile, and my politest Arabic. Rachid lets me work my way through my whole spiel and then just turns his back on me and walks away without saying a word. Major fail.

We ask Romain to explain. He does. Rachid is still not budging. Khalid has a go. Still not budging. Romain comes up with the excuse that Rachid thinks it is unlucky to swap cars half way through a journey. I suspect it is more to do with pride. Time is marching on and Laura starts brandishing her schedule, so we give in and all bundle into the car.

In order to film the conversation, Alicia is in the back seat with the camera, covered in a blanket while Séamas does shots of the car travelling. We ask Rachid to scooch down so we can get a decent shot. Of course, he doesn't, even though, Alicia, our Dear Leader, is huddled under a smelly blanket right beside him. It is annoying and funny at the same time.

Meanwhile, Romain is talking me through the importance of Guelmim as a trading centre. It rose to prominence in the 18th and 19th centuries and took over from Sijilmassa as that city began to fade. It is situated on the great plain of south western Morocco, Wadi Nun, also called Wadi Nul, and it straddled not only the trans-Saharan route but also the route to the Atlantic and the trading port of Essaouira.

The town was very mixed. Three groups dominated the trade: the Tikna tribe, their allies the Awlad Bu al-Siba, and the Jews. The leading tribe were the Tiknas whose influence spread down throughout west Africa. In fact, a Tikna became mayor of Timbuktu at one point. The trade network also became a family network, so cousins in Timbuktu would send their goods up to their cousins in Guelmim and vice versa.

Trading goods were gold, salt, slaves, ostrich feathers but also things like Gum Arabica from the Acacia tree. Ostrich feathers that travelled these routes were used by some of the Highland regiments to decorate their Tam o' Shanters. The Argyll and Sutherland regiment, for example, began using them in the 1700s. The original design for their head gear was a knitted Tam o' Shanter bonnet with a chequered border. Then they started to incorporate the ostrich feathers and to weave them into a lightweight cage which then gave the bonnet its height.

Slavery was a mainstay of the caravan trade. Not only the slavery that had existed for centuries, which was the bringing of captives from the countries of West Africa up to the North, but also a newer phenomenon which was the white slave trade. Barbary pirates would lie in wait off the coast to raid the European ships coming over to trade and capture the cargo and crew. The crew would then be brought inland to be ransomed or traded through Guelmim.

Captain James Riley, an American, was perhaps the most famous of these white slaves. He and his crew were shipwrecked off the coast and captured. They suffered horribly, were worked to death, starved and beaten. Eventually Captain Riley managed to persuade an Arab called Sidi Hamet to buy him and said that if he could get him to the coast, he would repay him and buy the freedom of his men for a great price. Sidi Hamet agreed, but threatened to cut his throat if he was lying. After a horrific journey, he and some of his men made it, were bought and rescued and made it home. Captain Riley wrote a book about his ordeal called, "Suffering in Africa," which Abraham Lincoln cited as one of the three most influential works that shaped his political ideology alongside the Bible and Pilgrim's Progress. When he got back to America, Captain Riley dedicated himself to combating slavery in America, before he eventually returned to sea, finally dying on his ship, the William Tell.

As we were talking, Romain was driving us up a steep and
treacherous escarpment. Sometimes he would fall silent so he could
concentrate on the road. He told me it was called the "Valley of the
Thieves", because bandits would lie in wait for the caravans and
ambush them as they negotiated one of the thirteen hairpin bends
that wound up to the top of the pass. I could see how simple it would
be, as there was only one way through the rock of the mountain and
it would be easy to block.

After we had navigated the dangers of the thirteen switchbacks,
Romain told me about the descendants of the slave trade in this area:

"Now there is no more slavery. But there is still an affiliation, there
is still a link. Here, the slave stays attached to their family. I don't
know if you know a very famous Malian writer, Abu Um Bataba, who
wrote a book called 'The Poor Child'. He talks about slavery and he
says that it's completely different from the Europeans, because when
an Arab or Malian family has a slave, that slave enters in the family,
he takes the name of the family. It's more like a Roman slave. They
are really part of the domestic house exactly like the Roman slaves.

"Also, now the difference is that the slaves, the ancient slaves, the
descendants of the slaves are considered to have a kind of baraka.
(Arabic for blessing)

"For example, the descendants of the slaves make some rituals, you
know and music and everything. All the white families go to these
rituals. If a white woman cannot have babies or has problems in the

pregnancy, she goes there, to these rituals and asks for the black population to give her a blessing to have a baby. And if, and when, she has a baby, the baby is considered part of the slave family, a descendant of the slaves. So, you see how a white man for example can become black, part of a black family, because of this blessing by the descendants of slavery."

We've arrived at Guelmim, which is still a thriving town and still has its camel market. Because of its geographic position and because it specialised in the caravan trade, for which you obviously need a lot of camels, this used to be the biggest camel market in the whole north west of Africa.

As we draw up, I get distracted by a cart of massive white radishes.

"Ooh look at all those radishes," I say excitedly.

"Yes,"says Alicia, "Marvellous. We are missing just one thing…. camels."

The market now is held in a large square just inside the walls of the town. We go in the big gate and I can see that it is mainly sheep and goats but with a few cows and a scattering of camels in the far left corner. It is almost all men, and I spot just three women in the whole place. The men are dressed in black or striped woollen jellabas and their faces are from all over Africa. Some of the goats are lying on the ground with their feet tied together, some are cuddled together for companionship, others are milling around, bleating loudly at their new conditions. Everywhere, there are little groups of men gesturing and talking animatedly, sometimes bending over to grab an animal and point out its good points.

Over by the group of camels is a trader, Ahmed, dressed in the bright blue robe that is common amongst the desert people (the Sahrawis). His eyes are lined with thick, black kohl and he speaks English. He tells me that he taught himself. "I talked with the people and then at night I went home and wrote the words in my book."

He explains that when he was a young man the market used to be held in a big, open space in the desert where people would come and sit and barter. They would spend an hour or maybe two or three, drink tea and seal their deals. He sounds wistful.

The characteristics for a good caravan camel, he tells me, were pretty simple. It had to be male and strong. The white ones were highly-prized though, as it is believed that they can sniff out water. So, they would always go at the head of the caravan and are called Ra'as (head in Arabic) as a result.

Now camels at this market are being sold for meat rather than transport and two of the women I spotted earlier are deep in discussions with the camel dealer. He trots his animal in front of them and Ahmed tells me that a fat camel can feed up to 300 guests at a wedding. There is no sale this time and the women go off in the direction of the goats.

A couple of metres away, there is another woman, who starts shrieking as the dealer tries to catch a rogue camel that is galloping up towards her. As I watch, he grabs the camel and forces it to its knees as it makes loud noises of protest. And then, before my fascinated eyes, he does something to it that looks a bit like milking but isn't. Suffice to say, he makes the camel pee into a bucket. There are more noisy protests. When he has enough in the bucket, he takes it over to the woman. She puts a cup into it, lifts it to her lips and drinks it. I am way too nosy to let this one pass and go up to her.

"Peace be upon you, my sister. How are you? How are things?"

"Thanks be to God. How are you? Do you speak Arabic? Where are you from?"

"Yes, I do. I am from Scotland but now I am a Marrakchia. Can I ask, what are you doing?"

"May the blessings of God be upon you. I am drinking camel pipi."

"Camel pipi. Why are you drinking camel pipi? What is the reason?"

"It is for my health. I am sick. I am very sick. Camel pipi can cure many things – even cure you of evil spirits (jinn)."

"I am sorry you are sick. May God grant you good health."

"Thank you, my sister. Go in peace."

"Go in peace."

Ahmed tells me that he thinks she may have cancer. I hope not.

I go off to get the bus back to our oasis for the night. There's a group of men waiting patiently at the bus stop and they say the bus is due any time.

"They were there this morning," quips Séamas.

The bus pulls up about ten minutes later.It is a small bus a bit like the small cross country ones which run near my home in the Peak District, and I get on and ask if they are ok for us to film. The driver says we are welcome to and most of the people on the bus nod. A couple of the young girls, about 12 -13, are told by their Mums to pull their scarves over their head and one woman says no, so Alicia makes sure not to catch her in shot. Meanwhile Séamas and Charlie are in with Khalid so that Séamas can get travelling shots. This appears to involve some serious stunt driving and the other passengers and I look on with interest as the crew car rushes past us, occasionally screaming to a halt.

"Khalid went past at 150km an hour. Catching the bus was definitely the most exciting thing on the shoot," says Charlie later.

Getting the bus has meant we have to miss out another thing on our schedule, camel milking.

"That was more important than camel milking," says Alicia, "You can milk a camel anytime."

Laura crosses it off the list.

Chapter Eight

"What leaves the head, doesn't leave the paper."

Nomad Proverb

Romain's knowledge about the trade was invaluable and before he left us, he did us one more favour by introducing us to his friends in Iligh, Aicha and her father, Imam, who come from a long line of merchants and who run a museum created around the trans-Saharan traders.

We approach Iligh through a long, empty plain. There is a thunderstorm coming and the sky is black. The town appears on the horizon, dwarfed by the boiling clouds and as we come closer I can make out the white turrets of a small fortress. It looks different to the ksars of the Ounila valley, as it is on entirely flat ground, with desert scrub all around and it is white, not the deep, reddish brown that we have been used to. There, everything was vibrant: bright blues and vivid greens, but here it is all brooding black and white.

No brooding from our hosts though, who have come outside the walls to meet us. They are full of smiles and hospitality. Aicha ushers us through the small door, and into a spacious, tiled courtyard where there is tea and breakfast laid out at the table. Alicia apologises and says we don't have time as we need to start filming. Aicha says we must drink and eat first. It is a battle of the Titans. I watch with interest, not sure who to put my money on. In fact, it is no contest. Aicha explains firmly that it is their custom to welcome travellers with food and drink and that we must drink some tea and eat her home-made pancakes with thyme-scented honey from her bees, then we can go and film. She is a woman in her own home and it is clear that this is not a request. Laura puts her schedule away, and we all tuck in to the delicious feast of fresh-baked breads, her own jam, olive oil, honey and amlou, the almond, honey and argan oil Moroccan version of peanut butter, the Rolls Royce of peanut butters. While we are eating, she tells me sternly that it is very important to do things correctly and to respect the traditions of her house. I am very happy to agree as I take another pancake in humble apology. Obviously, that was the only reason for that second pancake.I am a martyr to the cause.

Imam and Aicha are custodians to the museum which lies in the white fortress next to the house. As far as I can make out, Maison Illigh is a private museumthat they have created through their own efforts, based on the buildings and artefacts that remained here after the trade routes had changed and the town was no longer a stopping-off point.

The settlement was founded as a Sufi community and rose to prominence in the 17th century when it ruled the southern region of Morocco, independent of central control. It was a major post in the Timbuktu route and had a large Jewish population who worked the gold that came up with the caravans.

Imam leads us out of the house and across a yard, through a door set in a thick, mud wall. It opens on to the centre of the fortress which is a large square. This was the main trading area. Straight ahead there are three arches over a raised platform set out from the wall. This is where the scribes worked and to the right, there is a massive chain which used to hold the scales for weighing goods. To the left is a gate which goes out to the animals' section. The camels would have been hobbled or tethered here and the goods unloaded and brought in. At the far end of the square is a court with an adjoining prison. Swift retribution if you tried to cheat anyone. Standing in the square, it is very easy to imagine it as a bustling centre, with all the toing and froing of a busy market. I can see the scribes sitting cross-legged in their archways, totting up goods and costs of travel while the merchants sip tea and catch up on the latest gossip. I can hear the camels grunting as their drivers take the loads off them and they get to eat and drink. I'm pretty sure I can smell them too.

I follow Imam back into the courtyard and through a low door into a small room. This is the room of keys and there are dozens of them hanging on nails on the walls. These are not your average house key, they are giants made of rusting iron. They look like something from a fairy tale involving a wicked stepmother, a beautiful maiden and a tower. Imam takes down the biggest one and we cross the courtyard. There is a satisfying amount of flourish to the door opening.

We are now in an internal courtyard with four rooms going off it that used to be the living quarters of the ruler. He had four wives, and Imam explains that that is why each room is identical. There is a four-poster bed which was a gift to the ruler from Queen Victoria in one of the bedrooms. I find that strangely incongruous while my head is in the trans-Saharan trade. I haven't time to explore this side story, but I know it is going to stick in my mind like a burr. There are two wooden chests in the quarters and this is where the treasure lies. Imam opens one of them and hands me a book. I ask him the date and he says he thinks it is from the 1700s. In it are rows of numbers in Hebrew. It is obviously a ledger of some sort and Imam confirms that it is a merchant's log, presumably taken down by the scribes as they sat in the courtyard. He has dozens of the books in the two chests, written in Hebrew and Arabic, with lists and notes of goods bought and sold. I can't read Hebrew but I pore over them anyway, relishing my chance to hold these precious things and physically connect with the men who worked these routes centuries ago.

I'm so lost in my dreams of gold and precious goods that I don't notice the drama that has been unfolding around me. The local Qaid (local government administrator) has driven up on his moto to see what is happening but when given the filming permit, he pronounces it not valid and says we can't film. It covers the region but he says we need a permit to film inside the house. Charlie is sure we don't because it is a private property, but the Qaid is standing firm and Aicha and her father will not go against his wishes. Many, many phone calls are made. There is a lot of reasoning and pleading. Everyone wants the filming to happen, including the Qaid, but he is too fearful of the bureaucracy to agree to it. We try and try but it doesn't happen.

As we are waiting and discussing what to do, Imam shows me the old Jewish cemetery in the distance. It is about a kilometre out of town and the gravestones have lots of detail on them of names, dates, family and so on. He also shows me where the mellah, the Jewish quarter, used to be, but now it is just piles of rubble. I ask him if there are any Jews at all left in Illigh but he says that there are not, none at all. Another story waiting to be explored.

We are all downcast as we leave Illigh. It is a big piece of the puzzle of how the merchants would have lived and worked and we won't be able to show it to the audience. There is nothing we can do about it but it weighs heavily on all of us. I want everyone to be able to see those scribes' archways and the books that were written there, the great, old keys and the chain for the weighing scales. Séamas and Alicia are inconsolable and we have to make an emergency stop for chocolate.

The next morning, Charlie gets a call from the office. The permit was correct and legal, but now it is too late to go back. The schedule is our master and we must carry on. It is time to take on Zag.

Dinner that night is a planning meeting. The next day, our road will take us through to Zag, the last military checkpoint before we start entering the Western Sahara and a very sensitive area.

Just defining the Western Sahara is a task fraught with difficulty as you will inevitably offend someone and clash with someone's idea of what is right and true. So, I've turned to the BBC:

"Western Sahara is a sparsely-populated area of mostly desert situated on the northwest coast of Africa.

A former Spanish colony, it was annexed by Morocco in 1975. Since then it has been the subject of a long-running territorial dispute between Morocco and its indigenous Sahrawi people, led by the Polisario Front.

A 16-year-long insurgency ended with a UN-brokered truce in 1991 and the promise of a referendum on independence which has yet to take place.

Although under the de facto administrative control of Morocco, the status and sovereignty of Western Sahara remain unresolved and numerous direct talks have failed to break the political deadlock.

The Saharan Arab Democratic Republic (SADR), declared by the Polisario Front in 1976, is now recognised by many governments and is a full member of the African Union.

Home to phosphate reserves and rich fishing grounds off its coast, Western Sahara is also believed to have as yet untapped offshore oil deposits."

The disputed territory is bordered by Morocco to the north, Algeria to the northeast, Mauritania to the east and south, and the Atlantic Ocean to the west. It's a large swathe of land covering about 266,000 square kilometres (103,000 sq miles) but only has a tiny population of around 500,000, over half of whom live in Laayoune, its largest city. The landscape is mainly desert flatlands and water is scarce.

The Western Sahara question is an extremely sensitive subject in Morocco both internally and in its relations with Algeria and Mauritania. We had got a permit to film in Zag but we were not at all sure how we would be received there at the military checkpoints – hence the planning.

It was decided that Charlie and I would take the front car and the rest of the crew would follow. The thinking was that Charlie, who speaks good Arabic and who had been down to do a bit of research on Zag a couple of months before, would be best placed to get us through the checkpoint and I could also explain what we were doing on camera. Séamas fitted two gopros to the bonnet of Charlie's car so that he could film what was going on and then he also filmed from the other car.

Charlie and I have been on a lot of journeys together and normally don't have any trouble finding something to chat about, but this time we were silent for a lot of the way. Military outposts in every country are pretty averse to filming and I didn't want to face a situation where things got really tricky. I started to feel guilty in advance even though I had done nothing wrong and wasn't even going to try to breach any rules or do anything against the law.

I could feel the butterflies in my stomach. The road was another long, flat one and we saw the check point about half a kilometre before we got to it. We did a final conflab with Alicia. The plan was that Charlie would start talking to the guards but then I would get out of the car and go around to his side.

I felt genuinely apprehensive as it seemed to me there were a lot of ways that this could go wrong. But we were there and it was time to do it. Charlie came to a stop at the kiosk where the gendarmes were and rolled down his window as two of them came up to the car to talk to him.

The first thing I noticed was that they were filming us. They had cameras on their chests which were blinking away. Charlie was doing all the greetings and it was going well, big smiles all round. My imaginings of being blocked by hostile border guards melted away.

"Welcome in Morocco!"

"You speak Arabic? Where did you learn? They teach Arabic in your country. Very good. Very good. You are welcome here in Zag. You are welcome here in Morocco."

Alicia arrived and we asked the gendarmes if we could film and explained that we were doing a programme on trade routes. They asked us a few more questions and gathered up all our passports. Then, they went off into their kiosk to phone someone higher up. A football match was playing on their laptop and there were the makings of tea. They asked us to wait while they got a response from their boss and seemed very happy to have some company. We told them that we wanted to keep driving west and, although they wouldn't say anything definitive, they warned us that the tarmac road gave out to a dirt road and that from there on the area was mined. Alicia got out the packet of mini twixes and handed them out. This went down very well indeed. I asked them if they got a bit bored sitting out here and the answer was a wry, "Shwiyya" which means a little bit. The telephone rang and we waited for the next move. The boss said that we should carry on into town where we would be met and could discuss the situation further. We all said goodbye and got back into the cars.

Zag is not a big town. If you wanted somewhere to double as a wild west frontier town, this would be it. There is one main road, lined with small shops and cafes. Behind that are houses straggling out on both sides. A few chickens were pecking around and I saw one or two dogs lying in patches of sunlight. Sleepy would be a good word to describe it.

I was keeping my eyes peeled for military-looking men or police, as I thought that that was who would meet us further on in town but Charlie's experience shone through. He spotted a group of men standing by an official-looking building at the very far end of town.

"That's them," he said.

He was right but I have no idea how he knew because they were all dressed in civvies, black jellaba or white jellaba and just looked like a group of friends having a chat to me. They couldn't have been friendlier. We explained again what we were doing and Charlie showed them the permit. We told them that we wanted to go out of town, and to try and get onto the old trade routes. They said that wouldn't be possible as the area was a military zone and was heavily mined. We asked if they would mind saying that on camera as we would like our viewers to understand it. They told us that no-one official had the authority to speak on camera. We wheedled but to no avail. They were trying as hard as possible to be helpful and said there was no problem in taking shots of the town and suggested we talk to some "citizens" about the road.

Hmmmm. Accosting innocents and asking them to comment on security issues. This is not my favourite idea.

"Off, you go, Alice, Séamas is right beside you. Is your mic on?" says Alicia.

"I really don't think this is going to work," I say.

She just looks at me. She has broken me by now. The brumby has been tamed. I march off towards two lads sitting on a wall, minding their own business.

"Peace be upon you, my brothers."

"And upon you, Lalla." Lalla is used in Morocco as a term of respect for a woman, an older woman, and the nearest translation is probably Auntie. It's a very nice word and I like it a lot.

"My friends, we are making a TV programme for the BBC about the ancient trade routes and I would like to ask you some questions about the roads from Zag."

"Ah the BBC. BBC Arabic?"

"No, I am sorry, it is for BBC English." There is grave disappointment at this.

"We like BBC Arabic. We watch BBC Arabic news. It is much better than Al Jazeera. It is not biased, not political." I like these two boys more and more and am delighted at their praise for BBC Arabic. Many years ago, I spent two years working for BBC Arabic TV news, the first time it was launched and I am very proud of BBC news journalism.

"Maybe BBC Arabic, will take the programme and translate it," I say. "But, I don't know."

"Ok."

"So, can you tell me. Is it possible for us to go further down this road after the last checkpoint?"

They both laugh. "No, it is not possible, Lalla. It is only for military personnel. The road stops and then there is the piste. There are Ilgham everywhere on the roadside. Do you know what that is?"

"Yes, it is landmines."

"Yes, Lalla, it is too dangerous for you. It is forbidden. No-one goes there now. Only military."

I am really pleased as this has explained it very clearly so I just do my final check.

"Are you ok for us to show you talking to us on screen, this interview."

"Ah no, Lalla, we are soldiers. It is forbidden."

Back to square one. I walk around the corner to where four men are sitting round on little stools. They are all dressed magnificently in the white and blue robes which are typical ceremonial dress for the Sahrawi people – the desert people – from this region. The robes are called dara'a.

The Sahrawis are the people native to this whole southern and western area which covers southern Morocco, southwest Algeria and a large part of Mauritania including the disputed area of Western Sahara.

They are a mixture of ethnicities: Amazigh, Touareg, Arab and Black African. The dialect of Arabic spoken in the region is called Hasaniya and they are Sunni Muslims. They were early adopters of Islam, converting during the conquest in the 7th century. They are traditionally herdsman and traders, and used to travel freely across the boundaries that are now shut off and closed down by nation-state politics.

Fiercely independent, they held off Spanish and Portuguese invaders for three centuries. Their intimate knowledge of the desert meant they could use guerilla tactics to defeat much larger forces. However, in the 1930s, Spain and France joined to impose their rule on the Sahrawis and it is from that time that they started to settle in cities. The nomadic lifestyle became less normal, and the life in the cities provided an easier alternative to the harsh realities of the desert.

The Sahrawi identity is very strong and, as they grouped together in cities, it began to take the form of a nationalist movement which eventually led to the demand for a modern state of their own in the Western Sahara.

The way of life may have changed, but their traditions are still important, and one of those is drinking tea. Tea is important right across Morocco, but it has added importance when linked to this nomadic culture. The tea ceremony can take over an hour and every Sahrawi prides themselves on making a great pot of tea. When you drink the sweetened green tea of the Sahrawis, you must stay for three rounds: the first bitter like life, the second smooth like death and the third sweet like love.

The clothes are also very distinctive. The men wear blue or white dara'as, decorated with embroidery and the women wear melfas. Melfa comes from the word to wrap in Arabic and is one long piece of cloth which you wear over the whole body from the crown of your head to your toes. It is a little bit like a sari but with no naked bits and a head covering thrown in. They come in all colours of the rainbow but the ones I particularly like are tie-dyed cotton in the colours of the desert: red, sand, black and white.

My four interview prospects spotted me and invited me over for tea. I had to refuse because the light was starting to dim and I knew I didn't have the time but I explained what we were doing and then asked them what was happening. They were sitting in front of a marquee and were clearly dressed in their best.

"It is a wedding. Come in, come in, join us. May the blessings of God be upon you."

I love a good wedding and Séamas and Alicia had to trot to keep up with me as I dived into the marquee, no second invitation needed.

The marquee was big – about double the size of a British wedding one – and was full of round tables where the guests were seated. At the far end, there was a band of drummers, flautists and fiddlers. There was also a long table filled with sweets and cakes. At the back of the marquee, where I was, there was a whole row of young girls sitting on chairs watching what was going on. There was no sign of the bride and groom.

I went up to the girls and said hello and asked how they were enjoying the wedding. That was all it took. I was immediately surrounded and carried off in triumph to an empty table. A bottle of fanta and a giant plate of sticky pastries was brought up for me. The girls all sat down with me and inspected me minutely. My hair was felt, my hands grasped and looked at, my eyes exclaimed about. They were like bright butterflies fluttering around me and totally irresistible. They wanted to know everything who I was and where I came from, whether I was married with children, where I lived, how I spoke Arabic and what we were doing with the cameras.

I could happily have stayed for hours but we needed to do a piece to camera and so I went outside to catch the last ten minutes of daylight. My new entourage came too and we had to explain that they needed to keep very still and quiet.

While we had been inside the tent, Charlie had been busy and had found a merchant who used to travel the route to Timbuktu and who would be able to drive with us as far as we could go. Alicia, Séamas and Charlie debated long and hard whether we should stay the night in Zag or come back the next day. I played hand clapping games with all the children, "A sailor went to sea, sea, sea to see what he could see, see, see. But all that he could see, see, see was the bottom of the deep blue sea, sea, sea." Everyone wanted a go and there was lots of shouting of advice to each other and giggling. The team decided we would go back to Tighmert and come back fresh in the morning to meet our merchant and so it was time to say goodbye to all the children. Everyone wanted a kiss. The open delight which you are met with in this country if you take time to talk, or play, or have a tea makes it a complete joy to live and travel in Morocco. These simple interactions make me so happy.

On the way out of Zag, we collected our passports from the checkpoint and I drove back with James, who regaled me with tales of Brad and Angelina and other luminaries of the big screen, which I lapped up, and then had a quick snooze as he negotiated the passes down to the oasis.

The next morning it was a bit like Groundhog day. An early start for the drive to Zag but there was no nervousness this time. When we got to the checkpoint, which I now thought of as our checkpoint, we were waved through with just a good morning. Our group of officials was waiting for us in the same place and as good-natured as they were the day before.

The merchant was called Mansour and he had dressed for the occasion. He was wearing a dara'a of pale blue with silver embroidery which he told us had cost 2000 dirhams. That is a lot of money given that a primary school teacher here earns 2500 dirhams a month. He looked very fine and accepted our compliments gracefully. He told us that it was his daughter that had got married yesterday and he was obviously still basking in the glow of being such a generous host for the party. In many ways, it was much better to be able to have these routes explained by Mansour because he was actually a merchant who imported cloth from Mauritania, hence the magnificent dara'a.

He and I got into the car accompanied by the chief man of the town, the Pasha, who would be keeping an eye on things and we drove down the tarmac for a few kilometres until it ended. We were passed by some heavy military trucks and there were more coming in from the desert.

We arrived at a crossroads where one road branched off to the left and the other continued straight ahead. This was as far as we could go. Mansour explained to us that both these roads led to Timbuktu. The southern one went through Tindouf and was shorter but was uninhabited so there were no places to rest on the way. Once you were on that road, you were on your own. The other route went through Mahbes and was longer but there were little hamlets dotted along it, so it was relatively safer and you could re-provision, rather than having to carry absolutely all your food with you from the start.

However, both were now impassable. The military zone started here and we were not allowed to go any further. If we did go on, we would face landmines and armed soldiers who would not let us through. If, by some miracle, we did get through those barriers, we would eventually come up against The Wall.

The Wall is approximately 2,700 km (1,700 miles) long. It is constructed mainly of sand and runs through the Western Sahara and the southeastern portion of Morocco. It separates the Moroccan occupied, and controlled, areas, the so-called Southern Provinces, from the Polisario-controlled areas, the so-called Free Zone or Sahrawi Arab Democratic Republic, that lies along its eastern and southern border. It is, in fact, Donald Trump's dream.

The wall is composed of sand and stone walls or berms about three metres (10 ft) high, with bunkers, <u>fences</u> and <u>landmines</u> throughout. The barrier mine belt that runs along the structure has the dubious honour of being the longest continuous minefield in the world. Military bases, artillery posts and airfields dot the Moroccan-controlled side of the wall at regular intervals, and <u>radar</u> masts and other forms of electronic surveillance equipment are positioned right along it, watching.

Standing at the crossroads with Mansour and the Pasha, I could look out across the desert for miles. In the distance, I could just see the shape of a herd of camels, moving slowly, presumably the property of one of the Sahrawi nomads. The sand road, especially, was tantalizing. I wanted to set off and see how far I got. It looked so tempting, curving ahead of me to the horizon. How could it not be possible to still travel these ancient paths, through a deserted land? My reverie was broken, fittingly, by an army truck thundering past. The soldiers waved and said hello but they were soldiers nonetheless and proof, if we needed it, that there was no going on.

These trade routes had existed for thousands of years providing passage for goods from Africa to Europe. Now they were blocked by modern borders, modern weapons, modern walls.

We would have to find a modern solution.

But first, we had to go and have tea with the Pasha. It was like being in Alice in Wonderland, this place where the military ruled and there was no going forward, but the people were the nicest people in the world.

We spent a delightful couple of hours at the Pasha's house with him and Qaid Jamal and Qaid Rachid. A Qaid is an administrative rank of some seniority and so we were surrounded by dignitaries: two Qaids and a Pasha.

They had got everything ready for us for the tea party and the table was set with plates and forks, napkins, dates, and almond-filled pastries. My favourite pastry is called Corne De Gazelle, the Horn of the Gazelle, and is a thin pastry case shaped like a curved horn and filled with crushed almonds sweetened with honey.

We started off with milk and juice and dates and then progressed on to tea flavoured with saffron and Gum Arabica to go with our pastries. The TV in the background had been tuned in to France 24, a French news channel, but Qaid Jamal switched it to BBC World in our honour.

The Pasha told us he was from Fez which is where his wife and kids, who are at university, still live. He only got to see them two or three times a year. Pashas don't have any choice in where they get posted and I imagine that it must be very difficult for someone from the intellectual capital of Morocco, Fez, to end up in the wild west town of Zag, charming though the people are. A posting is usually for four years, but he had had to extend for a year because of the local elections in 2016 and had to extend for a further year in 2017 as there were parliamentary elections. That poor man must have hated democracy.

Qaid Jamal was sitting next to me, and wanted to show me some pictures of himself in his uniform on his phone. A Qaid is a half-military, half-civilian role so he had a very natty dress uniform. I told him he looked like a movie star, specifically Richard Gere in an Officer and a Gentleman, and although I am sure he had no idea what I was talking about, he was happy to get the compliment.

We left our two Qaids and a Pasha with many promises to send them a DVD of the programme and to drop in next time we were in Zag. We'd had a surreal time in this military town at the end of the road. In many ways, it was a disaster as our path was blocked at every turn and we could not get any further, but the kindness and overflowing hospitality of everyone we had met, meant we had actually had a wonderful experience. If ever I lose sight of the basic goodness of humanity, I think I'll just go back to Zag.

Our conundrum now was what route to take next. We did still have options. If we wanted to, we could drive right to Agadir on the Atlantic by a main route and then follow that coast road down through Dakhla. There is a highway all the way down that would take us by road through Mauritania, then into Senegal. From there, we could turn east and cross the border into Mali. This route would be relatively safe, at least until we got into Mali and then we would have to think again. It did not help our story though, as this was not a route that trans-Saharan traders would have taken. They would have headed down the roads that were now definitively shut to us. So, really, there would be no point in using that road. It would just add a lot of miles for nothing.

The traders of old faced enormous danger in trying to cross the desert but what we were facing was something intractable, modern borders and modern politics. Our whole aim was to try and discover the trade routes that had linked Europe to Timbuktu. We were on a quest to see what evidence we could find of the salt, gold, slaves and goods that had come from the glorious empires of West Africa. At the centre of this web was Timbuktu, our El Dorado, our mythical city of gold.

At every turn of our story so far, we had found our clues from the purely physical; gold coin minted 500 years ago and the salt flowers of the salt mine, to the stories of our storyteller in Marrakech; from the ancient book of law by Ahmed Baba el Timbukti in Tamegroute, to the beautiful, Ethiopian features of Hafida in the dunes of Erg Chebbi. We'd been dancing with the past but now it was time to change partners and recognize the part that today's world would play in our story.

We turned round and headed north, back to Casablanca, where we would catch a plane to take us to Bamako, the capital of Mali, to start the next part of our journey, a journey into the aftermath of war.

Chapter Nine

"How many grateful thanksgivings did I pour forth for the protection which God had vouchsafed to me amidst obstacles and dangers which appeared insurmountable. This duty being ended I looked around and found that the sight before me did not answer my expectations. I had formed a totally different idea of the grandeur and wealth of Timbuktu. The city presented, at first view, nothing but a mass of ill-looking houses built of earth. Nothing was seen in all directions but immense plains of quicksand of a yellowish white colour. Still, though I cannot account for the impression, there was something imposing in the aspect of a great city, raised in the midst of sands. And the difficulties surmounted by its founders cannot fail to excite admiration."

René Caillié, French Explorer, 1828-9. First European to return alive from Timbuktu.

When I heard that we had got the go ahead from the BBC to launch this adventure, my very first thought translates as something like, "woooooooo hoooooooooo yessssssssss woooooop huuzzzzzzzzahhhhh." My second thought was, "What about the war in Mali?" I have a few friends in Marrakech who do aid work there and I asked them what they thought. They raised a number of concerns over safety but were also worried that we did not avoid the issue of what was going on in the country in order to make a "nice" story, but reflected honestly on what we found.

The Mali Civil War began in January 2012 between the northern and southern parts of the country. On 16 January 2012, several groups began <u>fighting a campaign</u> against the <u>Malian government</u> for independence or greater autonomy for northern Mali, which they called Azawad. The largest of these was the National Movement for the Liberation of Azawad (MNLA), a Touareg independence organization.

Then, on 22 March 2012, the President was ousted in a coup d'état over his handling of the crisis, a month before a presidential election was to have taken place. Mutinous soldiers, calling themselves the National Committee for the Restoration of Democracy and State (CNRDR), took control and suspended the constitution. The rebels took advantage of the instability to overrun Mali's three largest northern cities—Kidal, Gao and Timbuktu— on three consecutive days. The MNLA declared Azawad's independence from Mali, proclaimed mission accomplished and called off the offensive.

To make this more complex, initially the MNLA were backed by the Islamic extremist group Ansar Dine. After the Malian military was driven from Azawad, Ansar Dine and a number of smaller extremist groups began imposing their own interpretation of Sharia law on the citizens. This was not the vision of the MNLA, who were a Touareg independence movement not an extremist Islamic movement. The MNLA began fighting against Ansar Dine and other groups, including the Movement for Oneness and Jihad in West Africa (MOJWA/MUJAO), a splinter group of Al Qaeda in the Islamic Maghreb (AQIM). By 17 July 2012, the MNLA had lost control of most of northern Mali's cities to the Islamic militants.

This meant that Timbuktu was now under the control of extremist Muslim militants who imposed their fanatical version of Sharia law on the city against the will of the citizens. It was a vicious occupation.

The new military government of Mali asked for foreign help to retake the north. On 11 January 2013, the French military began operations against the Islamic extremists supported by forces from other African Union states. Within a month, the militant-held territory had been retaken.

A peace deal between the government and Touareg rebels was signed on 18 June 2013 but on 26 September 2013 the rebels pulled out of it and claimed that the government had not respected its commitments to the truce. Sporadic fighting continued.

In April 2013, the snappily-named, United Nations Multidimensional Integrated Stabilization Mission in Mali (MINUSMA) was established by a security council resolution to "support political processes in that country and carry out a number of security-related tasks". MUNISMA was asked to support the transitional authorities of Mali in the stabilisation of the country and help it transition back to peace and full democracy.

In 2014, the UN Security Council further decided that MUNISMA should focus on "duties, such as ensuring security, stabilization and protection of civilians; supporting national political dialogue and reconciliation; and assisting the re-establishment of State authority, the rebuilding of the security sector, and the promotion and protection of human rights in that country."

A ceasefire agreement was signed on February 19, 2015 in Algiers but fighting and terrorist attacks continued. A quick look at the MUNISMA website shows that there are currently 15,209 uniformed personnel serving in Mali.

Mali is still not a safe place to be, with sporadic fighting and terrorist attacks a constant, especially in the north and around Timbuktu, which is where we were heading.

Both Tern TV and the BBC took our safety very seriously. To make sure we were fully prepared, we all had to make sure that our Hostile Environment Training was up to date. They also hired a specialist security company, Secret Compass, to brief us and to come with us. It also meant there were some very practical basics we had to follow. We would have to get to Timbuktu from Bamako, where we were flying into, by the safest route possible. While we were in Timbuktu, we would have to be very security aware. We couldn't stay in Timbuktu for too long and we had to go in with as few foreigners as possible.

The upshot was that our top team was trimmed. We had to say goodbye at Casablanca to Charlie, Khalid, Simo, James and Laura. It was like a scene from the film minus trench coats and trilbys. We had all grown close in our weeks spent together on the road and it was hard to think of doing the next part of the adventure without them. What would we do without Laura's organisation and one-liners, James' tales of celebrity, Simo's willingness to do anything and Khalid's insight into the Berber and Touareg nations?

I had especially loved sharing the adventure so far with Charlie. As well as being one hundred percent on point with the fixing, he had contributed loads to the story with his in-depth knowledge of the country. Also, he was my mate, and had listened when I shared my nerves at doing this TV malarkey for the first time, and then mocked me which is really what was needed.

Our flight out to Bamako, Mali's capital, was at night. We had a whole day to enjoy the delights of Casablanca which were basically going to the mall, dipping our toes in the sea and having lunch at Rick's Bar. When the owners built it, they copied the bar from the film down to the finest details, with the help of the studios, and it is actually like walking onto the set. The food is excellent too.

We left for the airport extra early to check in all the camera gear – six hours before the flight. Séamas was meticulous about his kit. He had to be. He was working solo as camera and sound man and we were going through all sorts of environments that were not friendly to gear. If anything broke or got lost or stolen, there was really no way to replace it.

Mali here we come! I live in Morocco and during that leg of our journey I had been to lots of places I had never seen before, met people for the first time and discovered this rich, trading history. Lots of it had been new for me, all of it had been enriching, but I had also had the chance to share some of the people and places I knew and bring them into our story. Mali was going to be all new and I couldn't wait. A brand new country.

The first thing was to link up with our new team members: Ben and Ismaiel. Ben was from Secret Compass and was going to be our security advisor in Mali. We had already met him in London when we got our security briefing.

Ex-forces, he has lived and travelled all over the world and had come back not long ago from Timbuktu where he had been working for a German crew, so he had first-hand recent knowledge. I was very impressed when we met in London. I am by no means an expert on the country, or on Touareg and Islamic extremist groups, but I know enough to know when I am being bullshitted to and that was what I was on the lookout for. I didn't need to worry. There wasn't any. Just solid, well-researched information and current, relevant experience and advice. Alicia, Séamas and I had been physically at the briefing in London and Laura had joined us by skype. I think I had better point out at this juncture that Ben is a very good-looking guy. He asked me to mention his firm jaw and well-defined six pack, which I am happy to do. He also has a good sense of humour so I am sure he will forgive our comments afterwards.

Me: "He's so taut I could trampoline off those abs."

Laura: "I think you are in VERY good hands with Ben."

Arriving at Bamako airport was like arriving in a steam bath. Hot, wet air welcomed us. We were met at the exit by our new Mr Fixit, Ismaiel. My first impressions were of someone tall and smiling with cool glasses, wearing a smart jacket and jeans. He was talking on his mobile but broke off when he saw us. He had been recommended as the man to go to in Mali, and he was to live up to that recommendation in every way. But for now, it was good enough to be met and taken to our hotel.

It was the middle of the night but I hung out of the car window like a panting labrador, taking in all the road signs and adverts and smelling the air. When we got to our hotel, we were inspected by security guards who scanned the car for bombs, as this was the main hotel for the UN staff and for foreigners. At the front desk things did not go as planned. They told us that we had cancelled the reservation and our rooms had been taken. This was clearly nonsense as we had not cancelled anything but Ismaiel handled it and within fifteen minutes we were in a hotel just down the road.

Bamako, itself, was not likely to be dangerous. There had been a terrorist attack in November 2015 by an Al-Qaeda affiliated group which left 21 dead but there were no imminent attacks expected. We were much more likely to get robbed or run over – I was to find out that traffic in Bamako is truly terrifying. Still, I thought it wouldn't do any harm to practise a little bit of security awareness.

So, before I went to bed, I checked out the basics.

Position of the exits.

Did the fire exit doors open?

Was there any way out over the roof?

Did my room have any way to get out of it if the door was forced?

Did the bathroom have a door that opened outwards (as this is harder to force)?

Was there anything I could wedge against the door if necessary?

I then made sure I had all the emergency contacts I needed to hand and that my mobile was charged.

We weren't due to start filming until the afternoon as we had arrived so late and that gave us time to catch our breath and for me to start learning my new language, Bambara. I love languages and one of the things that had helped us really get under the skin of things in Morocco was that I could speak to people. In Mali, my advantage was gone. The official language is French, but there were three other languages that would be useful to me: Bambara, which is spoken in Bamako; Songhai, which is spoken by the Songhais in Timbuktu and Tamashek which is spoken by the Touaregs. Sadly, I am no language genius, who can become fluent in a day, but I was determined to get down the twenty words that always help you to break through barriers and show the person you are talking to that you respect them and their culture. These are the greetings, thank you and please, words like beautiful and delicious and some easy questions and answers – what's your name for example.

I pried Ismaiel away from his phone and made him sit with me on the comfy chairs in the lobby and be my teacher. I wrote everything down phonetically on my iphone and then used my few words every chance I got. I think the bar staff where probably very puzzled as to why I greeted them so often and with such enthusiasm and exclaimed many times at the deliciousness of their sparkling water.

Armed with my words, I was ready to go out and see what clues I could find here left over from our ancient traders. We hit the market and it hit us right back. Bam! Noise, colour, heat, smells. This is a country on steroids. Everything is in glorious technicolour plus. The women's clothes were the thing that struck me immediately. Regardless of age or size, they all looked gorgeous. The national dress is a long straight skirt with a little kick at the bottom, with a short-sleeved peplum top and a matching headdress, all in the vibrant, almost violent, blues and greens, reds and yellows that typifies African print. The men were dressed in equally colourful long shirts and trousers. I felt so grey and boring in my tunic and trousers and scarf.

The market is divided into sections and we started off in the fetish or voodoo part where people come to get their remedies and advice from witch doctors. Dried bundles of herbs and mysterious powders lay at the front of all the stalls. But there were also leopard skins, civet cat skins, lots of monkey and crocodile skulls and even a dried tortoise. From my European perspective, all of this was bad. I couldn't bear to look at the civet skins and think of these beautiful animals being killed to feed a trade in what I consider to be superstitious nonsense. I tried to be more tolerant and understand and respect the beliefs of this place I was only a guest in, but this piece of the culture was just too far from my own. I was very glad when we left and went on to the more general market.

The traffic was insane. I was sure we were all going to get killed walking along the road as the green minibuses squeezed past us, horns blazing, at high speed. There were piles of nicknacks everywhere. I spotted gold and thought, "Ahha", but it was all fake. Big, glittery earrings and necklaces which would perfectly complement the bright prints worn by the women, as well as strings of coloured beads and stacks of red, blue, green, orange and rainbow bracelets. I noticed that one of the women selling the jewellery had on the biggest false eyelashes I had ever seen. The ladies here were all killer fashion conscious.

Fortunately, I didn't have any money with me, because I wanted to buy everything. I brought my mind back to the task in hand and away from this cornucopia of modern trade. Were there any clues here as to the traditional trade between West Africa and the North? Then I spotted him, an old man wearing a jellaba and skull cap, sitting down behind his blanket of goods and right in the middle? A great, white, shiny slab of salt.

"Aliiiiiccccciiiiiaaaa," I yelled. "Look, salt, a slab of salt." It was our first tie-in to the routes that we had been following through

Morocco.

I had not thought it was possible for this market to be any busier or more crowded until we go to the fruit and vegetable area. This was dominated by women sellers, most of them sitting with piles of one or two types of produce in front of them. Talk about feasting your eyes on something. There were so many colours and shapes jumbled together, my eyes were going to need a couple of rennies. Piles of green peppers, bunches of parsley with outsized leaves, lettuces, tomatoes, red scotch bonnet chillies, yams, cabbages, strange green things that looked like a cross between a tomato and a squash. Everything looked fresh and crisp and full of flavour. The chillies were so powerful that they were making me sneeze as I passed them. A woman in front of me was balancing an enormous gourd on her head as though it was nothing, chatting to her friend as she went. Another woman was making tasty looking meatballs over a little gas burner, which she wrapped in bread with chillies. Obviously, we stood out like martians at a football match and lots of the women called me over. My halting Bambara elicited gales of laughter and masses of goodwill. I learnt some new words for vegetables and heavily over-used the word "akadi" which means beautiful.

Our traders would have no problem provisioning here, I thought, as the food was so plentiful and fresh.

Alicia picked a place for us to do a piece to camera in the midst of the vegetable sellers. We wanted to do a walking one which meant that Séamas would be walking backwards and I would walk towards him, past him and then continue on. Ismaiel had Séamas' back and Alicia was looking into her portable monitor. I don't know how

Séamas did it in that place, walk backwards and film. It was so crowded that I was having to squeeze through people. If you have ever seen pictures of mackerel or herring swarming underwater, then you will get an idea of what it was like. I didn't help at all by constantly getting distracted by everything that was going on around me and not getting my pacing right. Séamas just patiently let me do it over and over again. "Work away now, work away." The intensity of the noise meant that Alicia couldn't hear a word of what I was saying and we had to pause to play it back for her. At one point, a very tall man carrying sacks of cabbages on his shoulders stopped to shake Séamas' hand. At another point, an irate lady called me over to tell me off for scaring away her customers and I learnt the words for I am sorry.

Timbuktu, had built its reputation on its gold. Back in Tangier, on our map of the trade routes,I had looked at the gold mines hundreds of miles away in West Africa where that gold had come from and now I was going to go and see one.

The countryside is completely different from anything we have seen in Morocco. It is flat with some jagged plugs of rock which are believed to give protection against evil. Ismaiel tells us that Mali is "98% Muslim, 2% Christian and 100% Animist." We had already seen evidence of that in the fetish market.

The rainy season had just finished a month ago and the harvest was coming in. Millet and rice are the staples in Mali. The millet is used to make couscous, pancakes and bread and every family usually has at least one meal of rice per day. There are mango trees on either side of the road. The season is two months away and the growing fruit are obvious. This area is famous for the quality of its mangoes. I also see a papaya crop in a small farm on our right and a bush with big five-finger leaves and clusters of fruit on top which I don't recognise. There are calabash trees dotted around. You can't eat their fruit but the gourds are used for bowls and vessels. There are almost no cars but we do see donkeys and a couple of horse-drawn carts.

We stop off briefly at a tiny hamlet made up of small mud huts with grass roofs. There is a big tamarind tree and a shea tree. A little girl has a doll tied to her back with a shawl like a baby. One woman is sifting millet to make flour as her baby plays at her feet. He has very cracked lips and I wish I had some salve on me. A group of women are breaking open what look like chestnuts. I ask Ismaiel what is going on and he explains that they are shea nuts which need to be shelled, ground down and then cooked to extract the butter. The butter is used on the skin but also for cooking and even for making chocolate. I wonder why that little boy has such badly-cracked lips if there is this butter available.

Back on the road we pass bundles of firewood and water melons for sale. Slightly further back, there are wicker things that are shaped like beehives and are stores for sorghum. There are also tables with glass bottles of what look like oil on top at regular intervals. They are not bottles of oil, they are actually bottles of petrol. These are mini, rural petrol stations where you can fuel up your motorbike or scooter at low cost.

The village where the miners live is clearly richer than the hamlet we stopped at. It has square mud huts with corrugated iron roofs and a few shops with awnings along the main street. We buy some kola nuts for the chief of the mine. Kola nuts are a mild stimulant and when you chew them and then spit out the remnants, your spit is bright red, which symbolises blood. They're the polite gift to give at all types of ceremonies like weddings or to show friendship and I am hoping they will get me off to a good start at the mine.

It is about five kilometres to the mine and I flag down one of the trike taxis which ferries workers back and forward. It is an open cart on the back of a motortrike driven by a cool dude called Drissa. He has left his earbuds dangling over the top of his ears, still pumping out music. I wish I could get away with that look. There are five boys and one girl in the trike, aged around eighteen. I clamber into the front just behind Drissa and Séamas perches at the back. The boys obligingly grab a hold of his legs so he doesn't tumble off as we leave the tarmac for a dirt track. I learn the Bambara words for stop and go. Vital.

Driving the trike is quite a skill. There are big holes and drifts of sand to navigate and loud thunks as we occasionally dip into one. As we are going up a hill through the scrubby trees the trike strains and slows to a crawl.

"I don't think it can cope with our European weight," says Séamas.

Suddenly, we turn out of the bush and into a wide expanse littered with people: women cooking and men wielding pickaxes. We have arrived at the mine.

I ask for the chief, Keita, and am directed to a group of men sitting in the shade of a tree. Keita is the family name of the tribe in this region and he owns the land that this mine is on. If you want to mine there, you pay an up-front fee – half of which goes to him and half of which goes to buy a sacrificial sheep which will bring the enterprise good luck and provide everyone with a tasty feast. I offer my kola nuts and they are immediately passed around. I have one too. Big mistake. It is bitter and feels like eating straw. I don't know what the etiquette is but I have to spit it out. Everyone laughs. Keita gives me Yaquba to be my mentor. He has roguish eyes and we are definitely going to get on. He speaks to me in French.

The mine is not full of deep tunnels but comprises many shafts going down from the surface to about three metres. Each shaft is worked by four men. If they find gold, they split it four ways. It is a community mine and will only last as long as the gold does. We could come back in six months and find it gone.

The miners' equipment is basic. They have wooden pick axes with evil-looking iron, bent needles at the head, shovels, buckets on ropes, and torches tied to their heads with bands of rubber. The most modern things they have are metal detectors which are used to scan the rubble for the gold.

There are lots of women at the mine. At the entrance, they were cooking sour porridge and fried fish, but further in, they are working the earth. They are in gangs, pulling up the detritus dug out by the miners in buckets tied to ropes. I have a go. It is hard work. The system is that they pull up nine buckets to be inspected for gold and then the tenth one belongs to them, if any gold is found, they split it.

The shafts are wide enough to get a body in and they plunge down into the darkness. The miners climb up and down them using footholds cut into the dirt. Alicia, having done an on-the-hoof safety assessment, wants me to climb down one.

"Are you mad?" I ask. "I'll break a leg, there isn't anywhere to put my feet." Once again, I have to question my own credentials as an Adventurer!

"Don't be silly," she says. "The miners are going up and down them and there are foot holds cut in. Look. You'll be fine."

My mule face appears. "Alicia, honestly, I don't want to. Do you really want me to fall and break something? This is crazy."

She doesn't answer, she just hunkers down in the dirt and then shimmies into a shaft and then the darkness, then shimmies back up again and pops her head up. She looks just like a Meer Cat.

"It's fine."

What a woman! I totally concede her the victory. Her cojones are way bigger than mine. I am genuinely impressed and think even more highly of her. Also, I can't wait to get in one now that I have been shown how to do it and when I do, it is as much fun as it looks.

Yaquba is keen to get me working and we go over to one of the more open areas where a group of men are working. I am given a pickaxe and sent to the back wall. The pickaxe going into the wall has the same feeling as that pointy, picky thing that the dentist pokes into your teeth to check if they are sound. I hook out chunks of earth and pile it up beside me. Some of it comes away easily but some doesn't. I am soon pouring in sweat.

For the next stage, I am given a shovel and I move the earth I have pickaxed out from inside the shaft to outside the shaft. I am a hot mess and feel overwhelming love for Ismaiel when he arrives at the lip of the mine carrying cold, fizzy drinks for all of us. Yaquba and I and all the other miners in that section have a coke break. Tastes so good.

Then it is the exciting bit. A guy comes over with his metal detector and passes it over my mound of earth. I can't tell you how much I want to find a bit of gold in the earth I have dug out. He passes it back and forward and moves it over every inch of my little pile. I am giving up hope and pretending to myself it doesn't matter when suddenly the machine goes, "Zhh, zhh." Gold, gold, gold! Yaquba beams at me proudly and then shows me what I have to do now. I need to sift through the earth with my hands until we spot the gold. I get to it. After about five minutes of me scrabbling around and peering myopically, the whole group of miners piles in and lots of experienced hands help me. They are so kind, they can see how excited I am and they want me to have the victory. Even though, they have obviously all spotted it, they keep guiding my hands and bringing in the metal detector to buzz for me until I finally get it myself. A nugget of gold. Capital letters and exclamation marks go off in my brain.

I have found gold. I have found exactly the same kind of gold that was used to make Mansa Musa, King of Timbuktu, the richest man in the world. There is the trans-Saharan trade right there, sitting in my hand. That gold coin I was so entranced with all the way back in the north of Morocco was made out of this.

I clamber out of the mine, covered in crap and feeling like a world conqueror, and trot off to the buyers to get it weighed. It is just a small piece on the end of a stone but they estimate it at about a gram. I buy it on the spot.

It is time for a piece to camera to show off this booty and we troop off to a hillock which looks out over the mine. Séamas needs me to hold the nugget up so he can see the gold and get me and the background in. I am ready and eager to go, flushed with success, and then disaster strikes.

I drop it. I drop the nugget. Panic. Inner mayhem. I can't see it. It could be anywhere on this hillock. "Don't move," yells Ismaiel and rushes off. He comes back with a metal detector and they scan round my feet until they get it. Phew. We do the piece to camera and then Alicia takes control of our gold. I am not to be trusted. I dropped the nugget.

That evening, at sunset, we go down to the river. The river Niger is an important part of our story as it was as crucial to the development of Timbuktu as a centre for trade.

The Niger is about 4,180km (2,600 miles) long, making it the third longest river in Africa after the Congo and the Nile, and the main river of western Africa. It is shaped a little like a boomerang and takes one of the strangest routes of any of the big rivers. The source is just 240km (15 miles) inland from the Atlantic but it runs directly away from the sea and into the Sahara and then takes a sharp right turn near Timbuktu and heads off to the Gulf of Guinea. This odd course was forged by two ancient rivers which joined together.

It is the northern part of the river near Timbuktu, that we are particularly interested in as it was the major source of water in that part of the Sahara and a trade artery between the south and north of Mali.

Of course, the river has many different names in different languages, but the word "Niger" can be traced back to Arab and Berber roots. It's another clue in our trading journey. Niger was first used by the Arab Historian Leo Africanus in his descriptions of the region from the 1500s and it may have come from the Berber "ger-n-ger" which means river of rivers.

A fact that caught my imagination when I was reading about the Niger, was that the first European to plot a large part of the river was a Scotsman, the explorer Mungo Park. He survived extreme and hostile conditions to journey up the whole middle section in the late 1700s and wrote a book about it called Travels in the Interior of Africa.

It was also where my historical crush, Ibn Battuta, saw his first hippopotamus.

"On reaching it I saw sixteen beasts with enormous bodies, and marvelled at them, taking them to be elephants, of which there are many in that country. Afterwards I saw that they had gone into the river, so I said to Abu Bakr, "What kind of animals are these?" He replied, "They are hippopotami which have come out to pasture ashore." They are bulkier than horses, have manes and tails, and their heads are like horses' heads, but their feet are like elephants' feet. "

We arrived at the river and parked up under a flyover. A truck had got wedged in the entrance. It was rush hour and the traffic was at its peak. It made the M25 on a Friday look like a country lane. I was sticking to Ismaiel like glue, walking, stopping and crossing where he did. The pollution in Bamako is obscene. You can taste the fumes and see the filth in the air. One guy biked past us clad in a full World War I style gas mask.

"It's because of the wood fires for cooking and the old cars," said Ismaiel laughing. "We call them FranceAuRevoir cars – once they are too old for France, you know, they are still fast and new here and so they say goodbye to France and welcome to Mali."

Fisherman's huts line the river. It is poor. There is a shop sign "Mr Plastic for all your plastic repairs." Nothing is wasted. Kids are getting washed at a water pump by their mothers and there is an elegant, veiled woman selling fresh dumplings. The earth is cultivated right down to the water's edge with perfectly-hoed rows of vegetables. There is even a small tannery.

The sunset is an African cliché. Golden light floods the river and a sole fisherman punts his long, wooden pirogue perfectly in front of the sun as a flock of birds takes flight. Séamas wants a shot of me on the opposite side of the bridge. There is a pavement there. However, I have observed that it is not used by pedestrians but is the motorbike lane, which means if I cross over there and stand looking wistfully over the water, I will be killed. I voice this and can see Séamas and Alicia seriously weighing up whether it is worth losing me to get the shot.

Given that we have not been able to follow our trade routes across the Sahara, it would be ideal to travel up to Timbuktu by river. The journey takes about three days. However, this route is also blocked to us. We are a tempting target and if we were to spend three days on a slow boat, it would be easy for anyone who was minded to attack or kidnap us, to waylay us at any point.

The reality is that, with the current situation in Mali, the only safe way for us to get to Timbuktu is under UN protection on a UN flight. Ben has good UN contacts here and thinks he can get us on one of the planes associated with the World Food Programme.

Early the next morning we head to the airport. We can't film because of security. There are armed guards on the entrance but the x-ray machine doesn't work and we are waved through without any checks of our big equipment boxes and bags. Séamas is taking the bare minimum of kit with him to Timbuktu as we have a strict weight limit on the UN plane. There are lots of uniformed UN personnel waiting in the airport. They are mainly Swedes from what I can see, although there are a few with another flag on their uniforms that I don't recognize. We hang around for a long time while Ben does his thing at the desk and then the word comes that we can go through.

We cross the tarmac to a propeller plane standing at the end of the runway. Our bags are all out on the ground and we have to identify them. We are greeted at the steps by the air hostess. We take our seats, she does the safety briefing, the captain says a few words and we take off.

Half an hour into the flight and Alicia is sound asleep. I poke Séamas.

"Séamas, Séamas," I say, "Look, the air hostess is flying the plane!"

I am not a good flier so this is causing me some alarm. Is that a thing on UN flights, letting the hostess drive?

"Alice, do you think she's an air hostess just because she's an attractive woman? She is the first lieutenant. What does that say about you? Shameful stereotyping!"

He is crowing with delight. Flapping his big crow wings all around the cabin.

I try to think of mitigating circumstances. There aren't any. Dammit.

"Yep. You'd better put that in the book," he says.

My shame is brought up many times over the next few days.

Underneath us is miles of red desert punctuated with some vegetation. We fly above the Niger and follow its course. It is massive, stretching out into what looks like a lake at one point. The water is almost the same colour as the desert, a reddish brown. Later it goes blue and there are strips of forest along its edge. Finally, it spreads into a delta, water is everywhere.

We taxi down the runway and as we get off I can feel myself blushing as I go past the air hostess/first lieutenant and walk down the stairs. We are here. We cross the tarmac and there is the sign:

"Welcome to Timbuktu"

Chapter Ten

"The houses of Timbuktu are huts made of clay-covered <u>wattles</u> with thatched roofs. In the centre of the city is a temple built of stone and mortar by an architect named Granata, and in addition there is a large palace, constructed by the same architect, where the king lives.

There are many wells containing sweet water in Timbuktu; and in addition, when the Niger is in flood canals deliver the water to the city. Grain and animals are abundant, so that the consumption of milk and butter is considerable. But salt is in very short supply because it is carried here from Tegaza, some 500 miles from Timbuktu. The king has a rich treasure of coins and gold ingots. One of these weighs 970 pounds."

Leo Africanus, History and Description of Africa, 1600

The airport is small and run down. Ismaiel immediately greets ten people and I get the feeling he knows everyone in Timbuktu. Everything seems pretty relaxed but that changes immediately we drive out. There are armed guards and soldiers everywhere. They have set up baffles at regular junctions along the road so that you can't just drive at full speed. The barriers encroach across about half the road and are sandbagged and with barbed wire on top. A couple of tanks are standing at the side. We are waved through with no problems. There's lots of civilian traffic. Women carrying large bundles on their heads walk towards town and some very impressively robed and turbaned Touaregs rev past on their motorbikes. The most exciting form of transport, though, is the donkey carts. They are 3-donkey deluxe vehicles: donkey 3x4s. They are carrying towering loads of hay and trotting along at quite a pace. I make a silent vow to get a lift on one at some point.

Before we even realised that we have entered Timbuktu, we are at the hotel. It's an anti-climax. Where is my city of gold? I supress these disloyal thoughts and bring my mind back to the present. Ben is going to give us our security briefing and then we are going to meet up with our security escort.

The Foreign Office warns against all travel to Timbuktu following its occupation by the Touareg nationalists and subsequently by the Islamic extremists in 2012. The whole of northern Mali is in the red zone. The danger is terrorist attacks and kidnap. Just two weeks before we flew in, there was a terrorist rocket attack on the airport. We were still in Morocco but when Tern TV and the BBC heard of this, we were asked to confirm again that we were happy to travel to Timbuktu and film there.

For me, my main worry was kidnap. I don't want my life to end horribly in an orange jumpsuit with my last moments being videoed for extremist propaganda and the entertainment of people who watch these things. On our Hostile Environments course, which was held – ironically – in Tunbridge Wells, we had done several simulations of being taken hostage. Even when you are doing a course and you know it is make believe, having a sack put over your head and being dragged into a shed, screamed at in a language you don't understand and manhandled and threatened is pretty intimidating.

The most sobering thing on the course, though, was the talk from Camilla Carr, an aid worker in Chechnya, who had been taken hostage by the Chechens in 1997 and kept captive with her boyfriend Jon James for 14 months. They were beaten, starved, kept in a tiny cell and Camilla was repeatedly raped. Thank God, they were released alive. Their ransom was paid. At around that time three British engineers who were kidnapped were beheaded. She had come to talk to us about survival strategies if any of us found ourselves in that situation. It was completely harrowing and I could hardly bear to listen to what she had to say. She has written a book, "The sky is always there; surviving a kidnap in Chechnya," and I felt terrible for not buying it to show her my support for what she had endured but I just couldn't. I knew if I read it, it would haunt me. We were told by the course leaders that there were two types of kidnap: economic and political. If it was economic we might get freed if the ransom was paid, but if it was political there was no chance whatsoever. Kidnap in Timbuktu was likely to be economic as the tourist economy had been totally destroyed by the occupation. The most likely scenario would be that we could be taken by a gang looking for easy money and then sold on to Al Qaeda to do what they liked with.

After that section of the course, I stayed behind to ask a couple of questions.

1. What do you do if you are raped? The answer was that you do not resist at all and that you make every effort for it not to be a violent rape. You must try and preserve your health at all costs. So, avoid antagonising the attackers and getting a beating as well.

2. If you know the kidnappers' language, should you let them know so that you can try and build a rapport? The reply was "ideally not" but that it was very likely that the kidnappers would look through your social media, so don't get caught in a lie. Play stupid.

All of this was in the back of my mind as we gathered round for our security briefing. Ben was very reassuring.

"Welcome to Timbuktu. We've had to stop just briefly to pick up our security detail for the rest of our time here, but it's also a good chance to give you a briefing about the security situation. It's a lot better than it has been in the past, during the crisis, but that's still not to say it's completely safe. Only two weeks ago there was a major rocket attack on the airport by the local insurgents and so it's quite jittery at the moment and they're very, very keen that we travel around with a full Malian army security detail to look after us.

So, we'll meet those guys in a second but in the meantime, let's just talk about a few procedures that we want to follow when we're in Timbuktu."

He then drew us a simple, clear map to orientate us. It was a heart shape for the city with the roads cutting through it.

"The river Niger runs right down at the bottom here, and there's an interconnecting road that runs north south. It's about five miles from here to the river. From the airport, we crossed the Ghaddafi canal right there. We are staying, here, at the Auberge de Desert.

"About 400 metres to our north is the big MUNISMA base, the main base is outside at the airport. Basically, the old part of Timbuktu, the medieval heart of the city is right here. It's just straight up that road and you've got the Sankore mosque here, you've got the other main mosque there and the market in the middle.

"If anything happens to us while we're here or out in town, we go straight for the MUNISMA base. They know us, they're expecting us. Timbuktu is within a bubble. It's within a security cordon and that cordon is incredibly good. That's why, when, two weeks ago, the insurgents launched their rocket attack, they did it from miles away because they didn't actually want to come into Timbuktu itself."

Me: "When we're out and about in the city, is there anything we need to be aware of?"

Ben: "I want everyone to stick together really. Not to go wandering off. Most of the incidents in the past six months have been banditry... there is a small threat of kidnap.

"Also, I always carry a full medical kit. The main things I've got in here are a complete trauma kit and also a bunch of communications.

"The other thing that I want you guys to do is carry your first field dressing and a tourniquet at all times. This is more important when we go out of the city when we're operating with the UN and when things get slightly hairier. Yeah can you pop one of those in your pocket. Same for you, here we go."

With that, he handed us all out a tourniquet and a couple of trauma dressings. I put mine in my backpack. I had been taught to use them during the course and ran through the procedure again in my head. We had also been issued with body armour and helmets but we would only need them when we left the city.

The last things he told us was that we would avoid any dodgy areas of town and that we would have to obey a strict curfew. We must be in the hotel during the hours of darkness.

It was clear that Ben absolutely knew what he was talking about and I knew that he would not take any risks. Our first job, before we could go out into the city and start exploring, was to pay our respects to the Army Chief.

The base was just off a roundabout and we went in past couple of soldiers who were having a cup of tea and watching a soap opera. So far, so relaxed. The Chief was a large man, very smart in his fatigues but incongruously sporting enormous silver rings on several of his fingers. They looked Touareg in design.

Ismaiel was leading our delegation and it was fascinating to watch him. Up until that point he had been a jolly, loud, flamboyant figure, making friends everywhere he went and always talking and laughing. In front of the Chief, though, he became quiet and submissive, very much the non-threatening supplicant to the Chief's top dog. I had no idea what they were saying but by the end of the meeting we had gathered another two guards from the Malian army who we were to pay and also feed.

Our security contingent was with us all through the trip. They did a great job. Sometimes I would be walking along a street being filmed and I would catch sight of one of them following me from the corner of my eye. Or I would be talking to a contributor and I would look up and one of them would be on the roof, scanning the surroundings.

At last, finally it was time to go into the city.

It's a sleepy, small town. Wide, dusty streets with little shops on either side selling random plastic things. There are some cars but more motorbikes and donkeys. Most people seem to be walking. I soon find out that it takes about two minutes to get everywhere here. Nothing is very far. The colour is overwhelmingly a silvery, grey sand. It is a backdrop to the colourful clothes of the Timbuktuans: African prints and Touareg robes.

We drive up near to the Sankore mosque and madrassa which is at the centre of the city and is our symbolic arrival point. Alicia and Séamas leap out of the car and go ahead to scout it out. I am forced to stay behind, chomping at the bit and not peeking, because they want to set up the cameras so they can genuinely get my first reactions.

The sky is bright blue as I walk up a narrow alley and suddenly there it is, this strange, clay edifice, like nothing I have ever seen before. Its walls are made of mud with wooden poles sticking out of them – the inner scaffolding. The minarets look a little bit like elongated beehives. This is it. The centre of town, just behind the main square. This where the merchants would have come to pray after making it safely out of the desert. Now, there are just a few children playing with an iron hoop. It is calm and ancient and feels unchanged, a rock that has let history, in all its turbulence, wash over it. I walk up the side of it, trailing my hand against the wall, touching history.

I am thrilled to be here. Thrilled to finally be at the heart of the myth. I am in the "furtherest place on earth."

The top of the mosque complex opens out on to the main square. It is big – about the size of Trafalgar Square I think. A few people are walking across it and some kids are playing football at the far end but I barely see them. What I see is the square as it would have been in the time of Mansa Musa.

It is full of people and small shops, animals and piles of goods. Some camels are being loaded with sacks of gold to make the journey north. A bale of ostrich feathers falls and splits open, scattering feathers everywhere. The merchants are in blue Touareg robes and black turbans with their veils drawn across their faces, arguing loudly with each other, slapping hands in a ritual of deal making. In one corner a temporary cafe is doing a roaring trade, doling out the sweet, hot tea that keeps you going in the heat. A white camel breaks free and races towards the vegetable stall, creating havoc. A tall, slim, young woman sashays past with a full basket on her head, enjoying the attention of the tea drinkers. The far corner, though, tells a much sadder story. A line of slaves is waiting, their eyes downcast, with no hope for future happiness and no knowledge of what will happen to them.

I am brought back to the present with a jolt as we need to do some filming. I talk to the camera for a bit about my first impressions and then I spot a lone tree at the edge of the square, where it meets an alley. Now, I have this permanent fantasy of sitting under an African tree, dreaming my life away. It stays with me even though I never seem to get the time to act it out. When I cycled from Cairo to Cape Town as a competitor in the Tour d'Afrique, it is what I had in mind. Why I had that in mind when I was embarking on the longest bike race in the world, I have no idea. But I did. Needless to say (the clue is in the words, "bike race"), I was disappointed. This tree in the main square of Timbuktu was perfect. It was a solo tree, with a flat surface underneath it, casting an ideal amount of shade. I plonked myself down on the dirt and Séamas did some shots of me reading my journal. I even dozed a little.

It was a temporary, but blissful, respite. We had a lot to discover in our city of gold. We headed to the market, but on the way Ismaiel stopped us and led us into an old courtyard with a tree in the middle of it whose branches reached right down to the ground, creating a natural fence.

"This is Baktu's well, the old slave woman's well. Come, come," he said.

The legend is that there was an old, slave woman called Baktu. She was the guardian of a well, where thirsty travellers used to stop with their animals for water. The sweetness of the well water and her hospitality meant that everyone who passed wanted to drink and rest there. A settlement grew around it that eventually became known as

Tin (the well of) Baktu and Timbuktu was born.

I fought through the trailing branches, and there in the gloom was a bubbling source of water, with a couple of ducklings on it.

In the market, there is a water melon truck being unloaded which has caused a log jam. Three very cool dudes in matching trilbys walk past. The market is small but busy. We are quickly swarmed by people trying to sell us things. Tourism used to be the main industry here but now, of course, it is totally dead, and so we are like honey to very hungry bears.

"If you ever want to end it all," says Ben, "Just run into the market and shout, "Mohammed I want to buy some jewellery!""

Down a side road, I see a Touareg in front of a large mound of salt and I go up to him. By now, I have learnt my few words of Tamashek so can do the greetings and then switch to French to explain about the programme. I have hit (white) gold. He leads me off the street and into his warehouse which is full of slabs of salt, carved from the salt mines.

His name is Natullah and he tells me that his family has always been in the salt business. When he was a young man, he joined the caravans and travelled north to the mines but the work was too hard and he prefers to buy and sell from his warehouse. The camel caravans used to travel right up to his door and he takes me out to the street to show me where they came down. Most of his salt comes from Taoudenni and that was a fifteen day journey by camel. In the past few years, camels have given way to trucks. They can make the journey in a couple of days.

In the back of his warehouse is a small room with chunks of salt, rock-size, piled up. This is for animals. It crunches under my feet. Outside is the "real" stuff. Large slabs of the best quality salt, about the size and shape of an average tombstone. They could be mistaken for white marble and are as heavy. I try to pick one up and can't. The best salt is called kamera and is silky to the touch. Natullah speaks of it with reverence. He is like a sommelier talking about a fine wine. He says that people come from Bamako purely to buy the salt. I ask him why it is so good, why it is so different from sea salt.

"The difference is that, when you consume sea salt, your body gets tired easily.
People from here who go to Goundam or Diré for work (where they eat sea salt), they come back with health problems, blood pressure issues. You can see the salt on their skin when sweating. This doesn't happen with this salt. With this salt, you only need a pinch and it would be enough on your food. This salt is intense, it really is. That's the difference, and that's why Taoudenni salt is the best. It's really good, you cannot even compare between the two.

I want to know how the modern-day trade works and, it transpires, it is not so different from hundreds of years ago. Natuallah has an Arab merchant he deals with. He buys the slabs from him; each one costs 10,000 francs, then he adds his cut and sells the slabs on to clients.

"We have clients coming from Bamako to buy this salt. Some people buy a couple of salt blocks as a gift for other people - it is really fancy. Or they take the blocks and go back to Bamako to sell them.

They consider this salt as medicine, they don't really consider it as ordinary salt," he tells me.

It is good business. There is no cheating in this business, it is straight. You just have to be honest, and you will be fine, you won't need anybody. You won't need anything else, you get your share and that's it. It's not something people bargain about, because they know it is good quality salt, they buy it."

Our salt story has come full circle. I think back to the mine in Morocco, then finding the pile in Sijilmassa market, seeing it in Bamako and now, here in Timbuktu. All we need to do now is the same thing for gold.

We head to the Grand Mosque to continue the search.

Saleh is a small man with a clever, mobile face. He is wearing a traditional robe of maroon brown, embroidered with silver. He is a professor and during the time I spend with him, several young men who are obviously his students, approach him respectfully to ask him questions. He is also an author on Timbuktu's history and customs and a story teller.

We meet him at the Djinguereber mosque, Timbuktu's most iconic monument. High walls of that same grey mud, punctuated by wooden poles, are fortified with rectangular towers, shaping into the elongated beehive-type minaret. Striking and strange. Saleh clearly has great influence and has managed to get us entrance into the mosque, something that is normally forbidden to infidels like us.

I take off my shoes and step inside to a cool, golden hall of pillars and archways stretching endlessly ahead of me. I can feel the peace and tranquillity of the place settling on me. Millions of prayers have been said here. They are in the walls. Saleh and I sit down with our backs to a pillar and he tells me more about Mansa Musa, Mali's greatest king, the Midas of his day.

"We are at Djinguereber in the Grand Mosque, the mosque of Mansa Musa, this great emperor of Mali in the 14th century. He came to Timbuktu in 1325, with all his spiritual power, his enormous power. According to legend, when his caravan got to Timbuktu, as the first camel arrived, the last one was still leaving Yamina in the extreme south of Mali.

"To show his wealth and his power, each camel was loaded with gold. He had with him thousands of people, and he parted for Mecca with fifty attendants who distributed gold generously in the Arab countries… in Egypt, in Saudi Arabia.

"He frittered away so much gold that the price of gold crashed.

"And when he returned to Timbuktu, he was fascinated by the religious character of the population. He came here with an architect, that he'd found in Egypt, an architect who was called Abu Es Haq Es Saheli, originally from Grenada. He told him to build this mosque that you see. It was a grand mosque with 20 metres of gold decoration. The architect was ingenious, he was from Spain and they found him in Egypt, so the construction of the mosque is a mixture of European and Egyptian pharaonic styles. When you see the two minarets of the mosque, they are like the Egyptian pyramids, the base is wide and it narrows towards the summit. "

The architect was clearly an efficient fellow and finished the mosque in a speedy five years, much to learn there for the tram-builders of Edinburgh. When he had finished, Mansa Musa, was so pleased with the results that he rewarded him with 200 kgs of gold.

We have come to the end of our story and I ask Saleh if there is still gold in Timbuktu. He shakes his head sadly and then beams me a smile as a great idea pops into his head.

"We were rich and we gave gold freely to the Arabs, and today when they are rich from petrol and we are poor, they ought to give us some of their money. Give the gold back."

It is coming to the end of the day and we need to get back to the hotel before curfew. Even more importantly, it is nearly time for evening prayer and the Imam of the mosque is getting very agitated. He needs us to leave so that the faithful can come in and pray in peace. There is a conflict here, as we need a couple of walking shots and at least one of me asking a question so that we can cut into Saleh's story if necessary. There is only one problem with this, I can't get Saleh to stop talking long enough to let me ask a question. He is so eloquent that I feel like a barbarian interrupting his flow. Alicia presses me, Séamas films and the Imam hops up and down with impatience.

Since the days of the legendary Mansa Musa, Timbuktu has been a goal for explorers. The early Arab historians, Ibn Battuta and Leo Africanus published the first accounts of the city in the 1500s but by the mid-1700s it had become something of an obsession for Europeans. It was the unreachable city. Mungo Park, charted some of the Niger but died before he got to Timbuktu. Major Daniel Haughton was commissioned by The African Association to find

Timbuktu. He travelled up the Gambia across the Senegal, but disappeared around Simbing. Then, in 1824, the French Geographical Society offered a cash prize for the first expedition from any nation to return from Timbuktu and the race was really on.

Alexander Gordon Laing was a military man and an old Africa hand. He was born in Edinburgh in 1794 and ended up in the Royal African Colonial Corps as a Captain. He was sent to the Mandingo country with the object of abolishing the slave trade in that region and encouraging other forms of commerce. He also fought in the Ashanti war. He was given the local rank of Major and in 1825 he published his book about his travels in western Africa.

That year, he also got married to the "flower-like" Emma Warrington, the daughter of the British Consul in Tripoli. It was a romantic whirlwind as Emma's father described it, "Although I am aware that Major Laing is a very gentlemanly, honourable and good man still I must allow a more wild, enthusiastic and romantic connection never before existed."

Laing may have been wildly in love with his bride but he also had a powerful mistress in the mysterious city of Timbuktu and just two days after his marriage, he left his new wife behind to go in search of her.

It was a long and difficult journey. He suffered all sorts of privations and misery; from thirst and exhaustion to dysentery and near-starvation. But it was treachery that was his greatest enemy. The man who he had trusted to get him across the desert, Sheikh Babani, betrayed him to the local Touaregs and they attacked him in the middle of the night. Many of his escort were killed and Laing suffered horrific injuries. Both his arms were broken in places and his right arm was nearly severed. He had a musket ball in his left hip, his jawbone was fractured, his left ear was split in two and he had sabre slashes across his face.

He wouldn't give up. He got his remaining men to tie him to his camel and somehow carried on for 400 miles. He must have had astounding reserves of physical and mental strength not to die on that trip across the desert and I can't begin to imagine how much he would have suffered, crossing what is already gruelling terrain, with broken bones jarring at every camel stride and wounds suppurating. What a hero.

Incredibly, he made it and entered Timbuktu on the 13th August, 1826. The gold and riches of Mansa Musa were long gone but he did find a treasury of old books and manuscripts which he spent 35 days studying in a house not far from the Djinguereber mosque.

There is nothing much to see there now, it is a simple mud-built house, cool after the heat of the outside and with a pleasant courtyard, but being there was enough for me. I sat down to read the last letter he ever sent. He wrote it to his father-in-law on September 21st, 1826.

"My dear Consul,

A very short epistle must serve to apprise you, as well as my dearest Emma, of my arrival at & departure from the great Capital of central

Africa, the former of which events took place on the 13th Ulto, and the latter will take place (Please God) at an early hour tomorrow morning. I have abandoned all thoughts of retracing my steps to Tripoli & came here with an intention of proceeding to Jennè by water, but this intention has been utterly upset, and my situation in Timbuktu rendered exceedingly unsafe by the unfriendly disposition of the Foolahs of Massina, who have this year upset the dominion of the Touareg & made themselves patrons of Timbutku & whose Sultan has expressed his hostiility to me in no equivocal terms. In a letter which Al Kaidi Boubokar, the Sheikh of this town received a few days after my arrival. He has now got intelligence of my being in Timbuktu, and as a party of Foolahs are hourly expected, Al Kaidi Boubokar, who is an excellent good man, & who trembles for my safety, has strongly urged my immediate departure, and I am sorry to say that the notice has been so short, and I have so much to do previous to going away, that this is the only communication I shall for the present be able to make.

"My destination is Sego, whither I hope to arrive in fifteen days, but I regret to say that the road is a vile one and my perils are not yet at an end, but my trust is God Who has hitherto bore me up amidst the severest trials & protected me amid the numerous dangers to which I have been exposed – I have no time to give you my account of Timbuktu, but shall briefly state that in every respect except in size (which does not exceed four miles in circumference) it has completely met my expectations –

"Kabra is five miles distant & is a neat town, situated on the very margin of the river – I have been busily employed during my stay searching the records of the town, which are abundant, and in acquiring information of every kind, nor is it with any common degree of satisfaction that I say, my perseverance has been amply rewarded - I am now convinced that my hypothesis concerning the termination of the Niger is correct –

"May God bless you all; I shall write to you fully from Sego, as also My Lord Bathurst, & I rather apprehend that both letters will reach you at one time, as none of the Ghadamis Merchants leave Timbuktu for two months to come –

"Again, May God bless you all, My Dear Emma must excuse my writing, I have begun a hundred letters to her, but have been unable to get thro' one; she is ever uppermost in my thoughts & I look forward with delight to the hour of our meeting, which please God, is now at no great distance. –

Your's ever truly

A. Gordon Laing"

By the time this letter reached the Consul and Laing's beautiful, young wife, Emma, he was already long dead.

The story is that after he left Timbuktu and was proceeding on his way to Jenné, he met up with a caravan of merchants carrying salt and joined them. However, they were stopped by Sheikh Hamet, who was known to be a fanatic. He demanded that Laing convert to Islam, but Laing steadfastly refused. Sheikh Hamet then ordered a Moor from Tafilet, who was in his troop, to kill Laing. The Moor refused, saying that this was the first Christian they had ever seen and he had done them no harm. He said they should talk to Laing and discover what he knew rather than just killing him. But the Sheikh didn't listen. He wanted Laing dead. So, he ordered two of his black slaves to murder him instead. One of them unwrapped his long, black turban from around his head. He wound it around Laing's neck. Each of the slaves took an end and pulled, and Laing was strangled to death.

His papers and precious journals are said to have been scattered to the wind in case they carried bad magic. However, some of his belongings may have survived as Réné Caillié, the French explorer, who came after him, said he found a copper pocket compass of English manufacture in Tafilet, which he was sure belonged to Laing.

Sitting in his house back in Timbuktu, I hoped that at the end as he was dying, his faith carried him through and his last thoughts were of his triumph in being the first European to reach the fabled city and of his "flower-like" wife.

What must Emma have thought, months later when her father got his last letter and she read that he had started writing to her a hundred times but had never managed to complete a letter. How she must have longed for him to have finished just one of those letters to her, or to have sent what he had written, even if it was only a scrap.

Two years later, the French explorer Réné Caillié, arrived in the city. He was much more circumspect than Laing who had made no efforts to blend in but had proudly worn his uniform and proclaimed his Christianity. Caillié had learnt Arabic and was dressed in ragged, local clothes. He kept a low profile and made it obvious that he had nothing of value on him to steal. In fact, in his journal – which is definitely a must-read – he says that at one point, he was in a mosque in Timbuktu and a worshipper came up to him and slipped a few cowries, which were a form of currency then, into his pocket, because he looked so poor.

Caillié made it back to France alive and claimed the French Geographical Society prize of 10,000 francs for being the first European to travel to Timbuktu and back. In 1830 the Society awarded both Caillié and Laing the Gold Medal in honour of their bravery and their achievements. Back in France, feted by the establishment, Caillié gave up exploring. He married and settled near his birthplace but he suffered from poor health and died of tuberculosis aged only 38.

Reading Laing's letter on the bench in his house brought home to me just how courageous these men were, who risked everything, and often lost, in their quest for knowledge. There was no Hostile Environment training or UN flights for them. They didn't have body armour or tourniquets and field dressings in their equipment. They set off into the unknown, determined to do something no-one had ever succeeded in doing before. I know that I am not brave enough to put my life on the line in that way, but as I sat there, I rather wished I were.

Chapter Eleven

"In general, the slaves are better treated in Timbuktu than in other countries. They are well clothed and fed and seldom beaten. They are required to observe religious duties, which they do very punctually; but they are nevertheless regarded as merchandise and are exported to Tripoli, Morocco, and other parts of the coast, where they are not so happy as Timbuktu. They always leave that place with regret, though they are ignorant of the fate that awaits them elsewhere.

At the time of my departure, I saw several slaves affectionately bidding each other adieu. The conformity of their melancholy situation excites among them a feeling of sympathy and mutual interest. At parting, they recommended good behaviour to each other; but the Moors frequently hurry their departure, and interrupt these affecting scenes, which are so well calculated to excite commiseration at their fate."

René Caillié, Travels through Central Africa to Timbuctoo, Volume 2

The trans-Saharan slave trade became established after the Arab conquest of North Africa in the 7th century. It remained a profitable business until the end of the 19th century. Twelve hundred years of human misery. Historians estimate that during that time up to thirteen million souls were transported across the Sahara. When I say transported, what I mean is that most of them walked. Within a camel caravan, the men and women and older children were tied to one another and then forced to walk. Many of them did not have shoes. The babies and very young toddlers were put in pouches and strapped to the camels. Around twenty percent of slaves died on the journey.

The slaves were captured in raids on farms and villages all across West Africa including modern-day Senegal, Mali and Ghana. Most slaves were animist, not Muslims although many of them would have converted when put into a Muslim family.

Gold and salt, those two mainstays of the trans-Saharan trade, both fuelled the need for slaves. They were used as manual labour in both sets of mines. We had seen the evidence of that up north in the Moroccan salt mine. Salt had a secondary link to the slave trade – it was the main currency for slave purchases. The height of the slave trade was actually in the 19th century when slaves were the main trading item across the routes. Their price dropped drastically and it was reported that their worth in salt was equivalent to the size of their food cut out of a slab. This meant you could buy a dozen slaves with just one slab of salt.

When he did his great pilgrimage to Mecca, Mansa Musa, travelled with a caravan that was 60,000 people strong. 12,000 of those were slaves, who as befitted Mansa Musa's status, were reputedly clad in robes of brocade and Persian silk. The emperor himself, was preceded by 500 slaves, each carrying a gold staff. I hope they didn't have to lug those all across the desert but just had to bring them out when they got near inhabited cities. Being dressed in brocade and carrying a gold bar in 50 C degree heat would be torture.

Having spent time with Hafida in Morocco and hearing her story and the story of her great grandmother, I asked Ismaiel, if there was any possibility of meeting with and talking to descendants of slaves in Timbuktu. He warned me that it was difficult as slavery here had still existed in his lifetime and people were sensitive. Finally, though, he founds someone who would talk to us, and we went down to his home on the outskirts of the city to meet him.

We met Mohammed Sise in his compound, which lay in a small hollow on the edge of town. He and his family had built everything themselves. The outside wall was made of wood, and inside, there was a tidy, sandy, open space, surrounded by a number of small huts made of woven, sisal matting. He was waiting for us with his wife and three children. They were sitting on some mats and a low bench in an area between the stockade wall and one of the huts. The tea was brewing. One of the kids was playing in the sandy space in the middle with some interested chickens and a baby goat. His brother lived in the back hut and his grandmother also had her own hut. She crawled out to say hello, but couldn't walk so I crouched down to meet her and pay my respects. As well as the three huts for Mohammed and his wife and kids, his brother and his grandmother, there was a separate kitchen and the piece de resistance a bathroom hut.

The tea was both bitter and very sweet: bitter like life, sweet like love. My impressions of Mohammed were that he was a very humble, shy man. He spoke in a low voice, kept his eyes down and was reserved but welcoming. After the greetings, we spoke in French. I felt uncomfortable because here was I, a foreigner and complete stranger, about to ask him very personal questions about what it was like to be a slave and what it meant. We were both doing this in a foreign language, too, so there was lots of room for misunderstanding and miscommunication. I wanted him to know that I was approaching him and his life with respect.

I had to ask some questions a few times to try and get a full understanding of what slavery involved in Timbuktu. This is a transcript of the first part of our conversation.

Me: "So, Mohammed, can you tell me a bit about your story as a slave?"

Mohammed: "I used to be a slave for the Arabs in the desert. I'd work a lot; I would get very exhausted when working for them. They wouldn't do anything."

Me: Did your Arab master treat you well?"

Mohammed: He didn't. He gave me a lot of exhausting work but I was obliged to stay with him because he raised me. I fed his cows; I brought water from the well and gave it to them. I was the one who did all of that. I was obliged because I knew nothing and no one."

Me: "I have a question, because I don't understand what it's like to be a slave. What is it like? Do you work and get money?"

Mohammed: "It's like this... for example you live over there. I walk by and you call me to come. I'll come over and I'll dig into dirt, sweep the house, wash things, and you'll pay me. If you do things for them, they have to pay you. So, I go there and work and when I finish I get paid. I live with them where I'll also eat and drink. I'm their slave."

Me: "I understand. And why are you a slave? Is it because of your father or your grandfather or ...?"

Mohammed: "I had been a slave since I was eight years old. I didn't see my father or my mother while I had been working in farms and gardens."

Me: "Do you know the story of slaves here in the Sahara?"

Mohammed: "The story of slaves?"

Me: "Yes."

Mohammed: "Well, what I remember about the slaves era, is that the Arabs mistreated the black Touareg a lot, they push them into doing things otherwise they would threaten to kill them. "They would do everything for the food, sometimes they would have nothing to wear, I saw them myself, they would carry heavy things on their backs. The Arabs would oblige them, and if they don't obey, it would get really bad for them."

Mohammed's mother and father were not in the picture, but his grandmother was with him and together they decided to go it alone. This was a little confusing to me, as I had preconceptions of slave "ownership".

Me: "Who was your master back when you were a slave?

Mohammed: "My master is no longer alive since the time of Alpha Oumar Konaré. He had no family when he died. I was his slave and he was my master. I couldn't stay in the village after his death so I came to stay here."

Me: "But I didn't understand something… was your master an Arab?"

Mohammed: "Yes, he was."

Me: "In the desert?"

Mohammed: "Yes."

Me: "And you got your freedom from him?"

Mohammed: "No, I got it by myself. I'm the one who decided I needed to stop being someone's slave. I decided to work and stay with my wife."

Me: "You're the one who decided."

Mohammed: "Yes, I'm the only one who made that decision."

Mohammed left his master's home and came to this place with his wife and grandmother. I wondered how he had managed to build so much when he had started with absolutely nothing.

He told me that he had begun his new, free life by collecting firewood and then selling it in the city. With that money he would buy rice and then his wife would sell it to the other slaves in the neighbourhood for a small profit. He could feed his family and any money they had left would go towards household goods and improvements to their compound. Now, he does odd jobs and goes to the market every day to see if he can find work.

I was so impressed by the life he had created. He had a thriving family, was taking care of his grandmother, and had a home which he had made. I compared my life with all its ease and privileges with his and felt ashamed of myself and how little I have done so far when I have started off with so much.

Mohammed's final words to me before we left were:

"Now I am no-one's slave, I am free."

Salt and slaves we had found evidence of here in Timbuktu, the gold, it seemed was long gone. But back in Guelmim, our charming, French anthropologist, Romain, had said something that had stuck with me:

"There was a lot of gold. But more important than gold was knowledge. This is the real gold of Timbuktu - knowledge, manuscripts. And people say that this is the real gold, in fact."

If, when you think of ancient books and manuscripts, you think of dusty tomes, curated by dustier librarians and you feel yourself starting to doze, wake up and get ready for a story as exciting as anything dreamed up by Ian Fleming.

At the height of their powers, Fez and Timbuktu were the greatest centres of learning in the mighty continent of Africa and far outstripped anything we had in Europe at the time. Students and professors travelled between the two and wealthy merchants bought books with the same voracity that Elizabeth Taylor bought diamonds. That heritage of priceless manuscripts and books had, over the centuries, been guarded in libraries such as that attached to the great Sankore mosque and madrassa but it had also been scattered amongst families and homes in Timbuktu and its surroundings.

In the 1980s a young librarian, Abdel Kaider Haidara, began his mission to gather those books which had been kept secret in the family trunks of merchant and nomad families and bring them together again in the safe haven of a library in Timbuktu. It was a hard sell. Families were suspicious of government and having guarded their treasures for so long, didn't give them up easily. But Haidara persevered and by the 2010s he had gathered a truly stunning collection of priceless historical documents, literary treasures and works of science together in the libraries of Timbuktu. Foreign donations came in from all over the world, including from Colonel Gaddafi, who it appeared had rather a penchant for Timbuktu and liked to give it gifts.

Then in 2012, the Islamic extremists took control of the city, and Haidara feared for his precious books. That is when he and his nephew, Mohammad Touré came up with an audacious scheme to smuggle the books out of Timbuktu and the hands of the extremists and down south to Bamako.

Over the next several months, Mohammad Touré and his small team of insanely brave volunteers, risked their lives nightly. Under cover of darkness, they packed the books silently into chests, loaded them into trucks and then ran the gamut of road blocks to get them out of the city.

If they had been discovered, they would almost certainly have been killed. Swift and violent punishment was a hallmark of the occupation. They risked their lives to save the heritage of a continent.

Before we started our quest to Timbuktu, I had read everything I could on the city and the Saharan crossings and one of my favourite books was "The Bad-Ass Librarians of Timbuktu" by Joshua Hammer which tells the story in full.

Now I was getting the chance to meet my very own bad-ass librarian, Bouyou Al Haidera from the Ahmed Baba Institute.

Bouyou met me at the entrance to the Institute and we immediately liked each other. He was small and impish with twinkly eyes and wearing a white skull cap with a little tuft on the top of it. The Institute had high-arched corridors, hung with large, brass lamps and something pleasingly symmetrical about its architecture.

It had been occupied by militants during the months that they ruled the city and some damage had been done to the building. I asked Bouyou what it was like and whether he was scared when the militants were in the building.

"Yes, I was," he said. "But this is my home. Even if I risk being killed where else would I go? I was born and raised in Timbuktu. I have to stay here."

To start my tour, he led me down to one of the rooms where the precious books are stored. The temperature and humidity are rigorously controlled to preserve the manuscripts which are written on a whole variety of materials: parchment, goat skin, paper, and even wood.

The treasures collected in the libraries of Timbuktu are extraordinary and I was delighted to be able to hold in my hand a book written in the 16th century. The script was difficult for me to read but I gave it a go, much to the hilarity of Bouyou who burst out laughing. It was the oldest book I have ever touched and Bouyou hovered around me, enjoying my pleasure and beaming with pride at the riches of the Institute.

In the next case, though, were a reminder of what had happened here: the charred remnants of partially-burned books. 4202 books were burned in total by the Islamic extremists.

Bouyou told me, "These are the ashes of manuscripts burnt by the occupying rebel forces in January 2012. Completely destroyed. They can't be salvaged."

I asked Bouyou why the extremists had set fire to the books – was it because they were "forbidden" texts, texts against Islam? His answer was a vehement, "No!"

"It was to hurt the people. These books didn't belong to either Timbuktu or the local area, but to the whole nation and the world. None of the books were forbidden. It was to hurt us. They destroyed mausoleums, tortured people and burnt the manuscripts. It was just to hurt the people. It's things that are difficult to find again. They were very valuable. Manuscripts from the 15th, 16th, 17th 18th centuries. It's things that are not easy to recover. It hurts the people."

Then Bouyou led me upstairs to take me through what had actually happened on that day in 2013.

"I'm going to show you where the occupiers burnt the manuscripts. I'll show you all the areas that were damaged by smoke. Here's where they put the box. You can see the black marks from the smoke. They put them in a box, put petrol on it and set it on fire. From outside we could see the smoke. That was the moment the French arrived. When they realised the French troops were here they ran away. Before that the leaders had never allowed anyone to touch the manuscripts. When they ran away we climbed the walls to hurry in here and empty the boxes. We were able to recover lots of manuscripts. (We put out the fire) with water, with what we had. We also found lots of boxes that hadn't been burnt."

Scorch marks are still clearly visible at the base of the grand pillar where the books had been burnt. I wondered why had the occupiers not touched the books for all the months they were in the library but then burnt them at the end? Bouyou had told me they burned the books to hurt the people of Timbuktu, I supposed it was a kind of final act of brutality. But what a waste. 4202 treasures of knowledge that can never be recovered, destroyed for what? To whose benefit?

There is another lasting and negative hangover from the occupation for Timbuktu's written treasures. As we know, many books and manuscripts were still being held by individual families in safe places. They had kept them for centuries, handing them down from father to son. During the occupation, many people fled the city and its environs, becoming refugees and ending up in camps. As their money ran out, they had to sell what they had in order to buy the necessities. Their books came out of the chests and were sold to the highest bidder. There is, apparently, a brisk, ongoing trade in them. Some of the manuscripts are being sold to collectors to treasure but there are also rumours that some are being bought up by those who oppose the more tolerant and exploratory philosophies of the Sufis in order to destroy them.

Our time in Timbuktu was strange because on the one hand we knew we were in an unsafe place and we were hearing stories about dreadful things that had happened during the occupation, but on the other hand we were all being seduced by the charm of the city. There is something about this place that makes you fall in love with it. Our tempo of life may have been a bit frantic but no-one else's was and it was a given that nobody would speak to us before ten am because it was just too early. Every person we met was delightful and happy to talk to us and help us. Even our security contingent, who should have been a little bit intimidating, were full of smiles and little jokes. One of them wore white gloves and reminded me strongly of a young Michael Jackson. The wide, dusty streets and quiet, ancient mud buildings were deeply tranquil and calming. It was hard to believe that there was still danger there.

Our days were, by necessity, crammed with as many stories and shots as we could get before we had to be back in our hotel for sunset curfew. When we did get back to the hotel, it was time for a beer, well a coke for me, lamb kebabs, and a chance to unwind and talk.

Ben usually started us off at dinner with a terrible joke.
"What did one female suicide bomber say to the other?........ Does my bomb look big in this?" and then the conversation would roam free. I always had to get as many notes from the day down as possible for the book so was usually scribbling away.

"Well, if we are in it, we are buying it," said Séamas one evening.
"That's three sold," chimed in Alicia.
"Can I borrow yours?" from Ben.

I laughed a lot.

Séamas. "I used to love the smell of Ambre Solaire. It reminds me of holidays."

Ben: "I think that is the most powerful aphrodisiac there is for men of a certain age."

I laughed more.

The next morning it was all business. We were joining a UN patrol to go to the river and visit the port. The river had been the other main artery for trade, and the conjunction of that and being at the end of Sahara, had made Timbuktu the great capital it had been. Gold and slaves and agricultural goods had travelled up the Niger from the south and east and salt had gone back down. It was the missing piece in our trade jigsaw.

Before we left to travel the 500 metres to the UN base, we all tried on our body armour and helmets. The armour is basically a big vest padded with Kevlar. It is heavy when you put it on but wearable and it will protect you from light shrapnel, knife thrusts, things like that. I don't think it would stop a bullet at close range. We wouldn't need them in the convoy, but Alicia was debating whether we would wear them when we got to the harbour as we would be mixing with civilians so the armour would make us stand out more and might be overkill when most people would be going around in their normal clothes.

At the base, we were met by a group of the UN contingent. It really was the United Nations and I had soon made friends with the Arab posse: two Jordanians, two Tunisians and a Yemeni. They were very pleased that I spoke Arabic and tried out their very best Classical Arabic on me. The Yemeni couldn't believe that I had visited his country. I had spent a month in Sana'a long before the recent troubles and we reminisced together fondly about chewing Qat and reciting poetry on long, hot afternoons.

Our briefing was given by the officer in charge that day who was a large, impressive Cameroonian. He took us through the route, the measures in place and the current security situation which he said was calm but unpredictable.

We headed off in two armoured vehicles with a third vehicle that had a gun mounted on the roof with soldiers manning it. It looked like a little tank. One of the vehicles was driven by Peter from Sweden who had told me that they were always on alert when they were on patrol as Mali was a dangerous posting and many UN personnel had been lost to IEDs and small arms attacks.

"Well you are all on edge when you are out on a patrol. You see what's happening what's going on around you, you watch people, their behaviour, things like that."

Our vehicle is driven by Kai, from Finland, with Camara from Guinea by his side. Kai makes me laugh (and flinch) by saying, "Shall I close the coffin now?" as he shuts the back door.

I am surprised by how green it is when we leave the city. We are within reach of the river and clever irrigation means we are driving through flooded eucalyptus groves, rice paddies and neat shambas (cultivated plots). Clusters of houses are strung out along the road and it is overwhelmingly agrarian. We crawl along at about 10km an hour. Kai waves to all the kids, who wave back.

The port is a marked contrast. It is a mass of activity. There are dozens of pirogues and pinnaces, which are big, wooden boats, drawn up to the jetty and constantly moving in and out of the dock. I estimate there are around three hundred people moving around the harbour. There are lots and lots of armed police and UN personnel stationed at different points, watching the crowd. Alicia decides not to go with the body armour and so I say a quick prayer that no-one wants to take a pot shot and hop out and into the mêlée.

Ibrahim is the harbour master and my guide as to what is going on. Most of the trade in this harbour is between Timbuktu and Mopte. I see mopeds, mattresses, millet and huge bags of rice being offloaded. There is also a brisk passenger traffic. One of the large pinnaces weighs around 60 tons and can carry 500 passengers. It takes two days to get to Mopte. The crew quarters are on top of the pinnace and the passengers are down below and both look pretty comfortable. There is also a little "restaurant" on each one where you can buy fish, rice, chicken, meat, coffee. Everything!" says Ibrahim with glee. The only way on is along a narrow, wobbly plank and I think back to my plunge into the river in the Atlas with trepidation. But I manage to get across and back without humiliating myself and providing the team with yet more amusement.

On the far bank, the ferries and large boats which take goods and people right up and down the Niger dock. We get in a pirogue to see the harbour from the river and get an idea of what is going on. Two of our armed UN escort come with us and sit at the front and back of the boat and we are given a strict twenty minute time limit to be on the water. It is so good to be out on the river. Water everywhere with birds fishing and wooden pirogues punting along. I am desperate to see a hippopotamus but Ibrahim crushes my hopes as they live much further up river.

He tells me that in the time of the Jihadists, as he calls them, trade stopped completely. It wasn't that they stopped trade from going on it was just that if any of the Jihadists saw someone with money, they would take it, steal it, so everyone stayed inside and locked their doors. Ibrahim, himself, had fallen foul of the situation and had feared for his life.

When, the militants had first arrived to take over the port, he had phoned the Malian army to tell them. Someone had seen him and informed on him. He had been seized and taken to prison.

He said, "Before, I was very weak, the Jihadists locked me up in a prison here in Timbuktu.
They really broke me. They punished me for having given away information to the military.
They still threaten to kill me. They say that if I kill or steal it is okay, but if I give away information about them, they will kill me…. Only God saved me."

Ibrahim had clearly feared for his life. He told me that he was sure they were going to slit his throat. After he was freed, he went back to his post as harbour master and he told me that it still rankled with him that no-one from the authorities or the army had ever thanked him for warning them and risking his life to do so.

"Since they took me," he said, "No one had come to look for me. They did not thank me or anything. I never saw anyone since then. Anyway, I did my job, I did my duties towards the Malian military, and no one ever came to felicitate me. Only God was by my side. Thanks be to God." I could sympathise with his anger.

Now, trade is back to normal and goods and passengers pass freely up and down the river. But I felt the weight of the threat of occupation all around me. I didn't like walking round the harbour under the eyes and guns of the military even though I was glad they were there to protect us. I didn't want to be in a place where there were so many loaded guns. This was an ordinary port with normal people getting on and off the ferries and pinnaces. Why should it have to be a place under threat and under guard? I wouldn't want to live my life in that way, why should anyone else have to?

Back at the base, Peter summed up the situation for us:

"Well in Timbuktu it's quite stable but if you go outside with no police, no military, the situation is different. (There are) a lot of criminals that commit robberies. They steal vehicles, they steal people's belongings. And there are also terrorist groups and they ambush with IEDs, but inside Timbuktu, touch wood, it's stable.

"I think most people like that we are here. They sense that we give stability, because if we were to go from Timbuktu, I think the Jihadists would come back. As long as we are here, I think that gives stability to Timbuktu."

Chapter Twelve

"Salt comes from the north, gold from the south, and silver from the country of the white men, but the word of God and the treasures of wisdom are only to be found in Timbuktu."

West African Proverb

Though not the El Dorado of my imagination, Timbuktu had begun to cast a spell on me. Its peace is seductive. I wanted to spend some time getting to understand life there now, the daily routine, how people work, the local food …. well that is what I told Alicia as I spotted a woman cooking doughnuts at the side of the road. I also love a good doughnut.

She was sitting over an iron pot which had a wood fire in it, beside her were a small pile of sticks for fuel. On her other side was the batter in a plastic bowl and on top of the iron pot she had a cast iron skillet with scoops in it – a bit like an egg poacher. She ladled the mixture in and then turned over the pancakes with a long-handled spoon. Soon they were ready and so was I.

Oh, the disappointment. Plump and juicy to look at, they were, in fact, rubbery, not at all sweet and had a lot of sand in them. I chewed womanfully, feeling the grit grind into my fillings, and tried to look delighted but my heart died a little inside.

Being up early meant we had a chance to catch the women at the bread ovens. We had spotted them all over town. The ovens look a bit like the minarets on the mosque, tall, elongated beehives, with an opening that we had only ever seen bricked up in the daytime. But in the morning, the doorway was unbricked and a fire burned brightly inside. Women came with their dough, much like they had in Fez, and then sat on a bench opposite and had a chat while the baker, who was also a woman, flipped the bread in the oven with her spatula. One woman left with a pot full of burning embers, presumably to stoke her cooking fire back at home. I also finally caught a glimpse of some real gold. One of the women, in the houses opposite the bread oven, was wearing a headscarf which had antique, gold medallions sewn all over it.

Further down the road, I could hear the sounds of chanting. Up one of the wide streets, there was a straw-roofed lean-to occupying almost the entirety of a narrow alleyway. Outside were dozens of pairs of very small sandals. I ducked into the latticed shade and found myself in a makeshift classroom. There must have been about fifty children there aged between five and twelve, both boys and girls. It was like walking into the centre of a hornets' nest. They were all chanting different words, at different times and different levels of intensity. New children kept arriving, slipping off their sandals, darting into the middle of the space and choosing a wooden paddle from one of two large, wicker baskets. They would then squeeze themselves into whatever spot they could find and get to it. The boys were at one end and the girls at the other and both were equally vocal.

It is a Quranic school. The children are learning the verses of the Quran which are written in Arabic on the wooden paddles. The teacher is sitting in the centre on a low chair and beckons me to join him. He is called Omar.

He tells me that he has been teaching at the school for 25 years, in this makeshift classroom in this alley. He built it with the help of some of the fathers and points out how the wooden poles hold up the rattan matting. He worries because they could get moved on at any time by the authorities and also because he believes the children need something better. But this may be the only education they get. He works without a proper salary and exists on what the parents give him.

Buzz, buzz, buzz goes the chanting of the children. I can hear one of the boys above the others. He has a high, clear voice and he is enunciating the musical Arabic of the verses perfectly. Omar calls him over and the others fall silent as Abdel Karim sings his way perfectly through the lines. Arabic, the language of the Quran, is not spoken in Timbuktu so I ask Omar which language he teaches in. He teaches mainly in Songhay. The children not only learn to read Arabic but they also write it on their slates, copying out letters, words, verses or chapters according to their age and ability. In addition to the Quran, Omar instructs them in the Hadith, the sayings of the Prophet. I have underestimated the numbers, there are around 200 children who attend the school and it is held from Friday to Wednesday with Thursdays off.

Omar's parting words to me are, "The Prophet said, "The best of you are those who learn the Quran and teach it".

It appears that most people in Timbuktu walk to get where they are going. They have to share the road with sheep and goats, which look remarkably similar here. Séamas and I have a heated debate over a passing flock – he says goats but I know from their long ears they are sheep. Google is invoked but convinces neither of us that the other is wrong. I am definitely right. There are a few cars and some trucks taking goods to the market, and there are plenty of motorcycles and of course, my favourite, the 3-donkey cart. Ever since I saw these carts on the first day, I had wanted to have a ride on one and now was the time.

Al Hassan was my driver, a dark, brooding Touareg, who initially resisted all my attempts to befriend him with my limited Tamashek, but eventually gave in, possibly through sheer exhaustion. Once, I'd levered myself up on to the cart, on to the spot where he had put a little bit of cardboard down for my bottom, we set off at a good pace. He had a frightening-looking stick but only used it to tap. The three donkeys were harnessed but none of them were bridled and, from what I could see, it was the middle one that did almost all the work. The one on the left also seemed to be pulling a bit but the one on the right appeared to be doing nothing, just taking it easy. Al Hassan told me that after he dropped me off, he was heading out of town to bring back the harvested crops. There was a kind of dual carriage way of donkeys heading in and out, empty on the outbound journey and laden with enormous loads of what looked like hay on the way back.

The Touaregs were the founders of Timbuktu, creating the city at the beginning of the 12th century. They are a Berber group and stretch across the Sahara. Traders, nomads, herdsman, desert guides and warriors, their society is distinguished by ordered "castes". In the West, they are sometimes known as the "blue men" this is because the pigment of the indigo turbans they wear, the lower part of which they also pull across their faces as a veil, leaves its blue dye on their skin.

We had been invited to have lunch with a Touareg family, Maya and her husband Mohammed and their children, and I was curious to see how this society worked, where the men are veiled and the women are not and it is said that the women hold sway.

The family live in a compound with a tent in the open courtyard behind the mud walls, and a house at the back. I could see work going on in the tent, but I was going to help Maya cook lunch so I headed straight for her. A gorgeous, glorious woman dressed in a pink milfa (wrap/robe) meets me. She is all golden and dimpled and we exchange smiles. In Touareg culture, fat women are celebrated for their beauty. When he got to Timbuktu, the French Explorer, René Caillié, wrote:

"The largest and the fattest are the most admired. To be a real beauty with them, a woman must have such a degree of obesity as will render her unable to walk without two assistants."

Maya's husband, Mohammed, is thin as a rail. Maya is sitting behind the tent in the cooking area. She has two chairs set up and in front of them are two large steel casseroles over two charcoal burners. There are a couple of basins ready for use and some stirring implements. There is also a huge wooden pestle and mortar off to the side. The goat meat is in one and the rice is in the other. Maya tells me that they eat the same thing for breakfast, lunch and dinner and it is always some variation of meat, rice and milk. I am ludicrously pleased when she puts the salt in, and when I ask where it is from she replies, "Taoudenni", real Saharan salt.

She has four children of whom, Ahmed at around 15 is the oldest. He speaks good English, which he has taught himself, and I ask him if he can do me a favour. I saw Malian football kit for sale in the market and I want to buy it for my nephew who is a keen player but I know we may not have time to go back. It also means I can give him a little bit of extra money. He is so happy to be given a mission. I explain to him that Jamie is about his height but is broader and that he needs XL. Jamie is not at all fat, but here all the men are tiny. He bounds off and soon comes back with the bright, yellow kit.

"Look," he says beaming, "XXXL". It is still pretty small.

In the meantime, I have been talking to his cousin who is around the same age, 15. He picks up the baby of the family, Maya's youngest daughter, who is rushing around in her stripey romper, kisses her and says:

"This is my future wife. She will be for me when she grows up." She obviously loves him and sits happily playing on his knee. It shows me the depth of family and clan ties here.

The goat and rice are cooked now and the last thing we do before serving is to pound the meat in the pestle and mortar to really tenderise it. Then we put it on a plate and go into the tent to where Mohammed has been working away with his sister, his mother and (I think) his brother. They are busy making handcrafts which they used to sell to tourists. The goat is delicious, very rich but it melts in the mouth. The men are all veiled and when they eat, they have to reach under the veils to their mouths. It is all quite a delicate operation. When I ask about it they tell me that the men take the veil when they reach manhood and that it is forbidden in their culture for women to see the men's faces. You wear the veil at different levels on your face according to levels of respect and respectfulness: high up is very respectful, whereas lower down is more relaxed.

I asked Mohammed what it meant to be a Touareg.

"We are simple men of the desert," he said. "We are brave men, at one with nature. We are herders and camel drivers."

Mohammed told me that his family also had a house in the desert where he kept his flocks and that his family went back and forth between the desert and the town. He used to work with the caravans during the season – caravans for both goods and tourists – but now it is too dangerous and the caravans have stopped. His work here in the city was in artefacts. He was making a silver and wooden necklace inlaid with yellow stones and pointed out the markings round the edge to me. They symbolised all the things of the desert: the camel's pads, a tent, a well and the stars. His sister was busy fringing a leather, embroidered cushion that would have been used for the camels and his Mum was working on a sheath for a dagger. The work was exquisite and, of course, we all bought something.

He told us that life had become extremely difficult for them after the occupation because tourism had been one of their main sources of income and now the trade is dead. The UN troops buy things, but there aren't as many of them as there were tourists. Life has got harder for the family. It is also about lack of opportunity. I look at young Ahmed, so intelligent and eager and aspiring and wonder what life has to hold for him in the future. A boy like that could achieve absolutely anything, given the chance.

The future was still on my mind as I went to meet the Cultural Leader of the city, the Chef de la Mission Culturelle, Timbuktu, Al Boukhari Ben Essayouti, in the shadow of the Djinguereber mosque. He took me round the mosque, pointing out things that I had not seen, with my untutored eye. He showed me holes in the exterior cladding and areas where the material had degraded. What I had thought was mud, was actually much more complex.

"You see here is the exterior coating, this is prepared with soil, beneath the surface there are rocks we call Al Hor, native to Timbuktu, used as reinforcement … We normally put Banko that is enriched with Bao Bao powder and Shea butter on the exterior. Since this hasn't been done, and with the heavy rains, the coating and the plastering have fallen off.

You can see here, there is wheat straw, and also what we call rice husk. We put that on the exterior, now you see it's falling apart."

Shea butter, beloved of moisturising creams, to reinforce the wall of an ancient mosque? Who knew?! The serious point, though, was that before the occupation, the city had come together annually to repair the mosque using the traditional methods. The guild of masons would gather volunteers and the men of Timbuktu would spend a day or days making the exterior of the walls good again, safeguarding their patrimony. During the occupation, the Islamic extremists had banned all public gatherings, so they had been unable to repair this great mosque. And their legacy lingered after, as people were frightened to get together in large groups in case of attack. I found it utterly depressing – the senselessness of preventing muslims from repairing a mosque – and a fine illustration of how little extremism and fanaticism really have to do with the religion they purport to be fighting for.

Al Boukhari explained that there was a silver lining to the cloud of destruction.

"I think the only positive thing that resulted of the Jihadists' occupation was that people have become more aware of this site. Because when they took control over the city, when the mausoleums were destroyed, and some mosques vandalised, the whole international community was mobilised, and the events were widely spread via the media.

"The people of Timbuktu have realized that their cultural heritage is a true treasure that belongs not only to them but to the whole world."

In practical terms, UNESCO has stepped into the breach and was sending over specialists in earthen building preservation to work with the local masons. This meant that the mosque would be preserved in a more systematic and rigorous way.

Looking ahead, I asked Al Boukhari what he thought would make Timbuktu flourish again, become the city that it had once been, or at least its equivalent in a changed world.

"Well, the city of Timbuktu lives off tourism. It is a culture-based tourism. Tourists come to see the cultural heritage and to enjoy the landscape. People earn their living through tourism, not only the tourist guides and the hoteliers, but also the craftsmen. Between fifty and sixty percent of the city's population are craftsmen. Tourists buy handmade traditional products, and this is what will revive and preserve the city of Timbuktu and make it more prosperous."

Until that happens, the industrious Timbuktuans are making the most of what they have. Local associations have been set up, partially with the help of foreign aid, to create jobs and prospects. One of these, is a women's co-operative supported by Endamali, which trains up women to dye the fabric used for the men's traditional robes. The cloth is called Basin cloth and the robes are called Boubous. It is right on the outskirts of town and when we get there, our security contingent immediately goes on high alert. They don't like us being this close to the open desert. It looks completely calm to me. I can see a few camels in the distance and a herd of goats munching away on the scrub. An idyllic pastoral scene. Nevertheless, they want us to get into the compound as quickly as possible and they fan out to put a barrier between us and the open ground.

Inside the compound, there is a whole group of vividly-dressed young women working and chattering at the dyeing tubs. It is a little bit like the tannery in Marrakech and I have to put on two pairs of gloves – cotton inside and rubber gauntlets outside. The women get me involved and show me what to do. I put two tablespoons of acid into a tub of boiling water and stir it around. Then I add the pigment and then I add the cloth and mix it through. After that, we hang it up to dry and then start the process again if it is a colour that requires more than one pigment. We do two colours: orange and green and we have to change gloves in between so that the colours stay pure.

When I have done my stint, it is time for tea and to learn about the girls. We sit together on comfortable banquettes with cushions, squashed together in a riot of colour. The sky above is bright blue and I can hear the birds singing. One of the women has brought her baby and he is lying on the floor by her side, kicking his legs up. The women are laughing and jostling each other but when they start telling their stories all of that beauty and light fades and all I feel is darkness.

Two of the girls, who are in their late teens/early twenties tell me how they were forced into marriages with the occupiers – the Islamic extremists.

"They married me by force. I had no choice. I really suffered in this crisis. If I refused to do anything he would beat me all the time. If we went out into the street without covering our heads, we would be punished. They beat me all the time. It was a really hard time for us. I suffered so much in this marriage. I suffered. I was hungry. I was being hit. It was really unbearable. It was very hard. Since then, I haven't got a husband so far."

She starts to cry and is comforted by the other women as the second girl takes up the story.

"I was also married by force. I didn't like him, but I had no choice because they forced me. When he saw me, he said that he wanted to take me in marriage. I said no. But then afterwards, they (the occupiers) came to see my parents. They also said no. But then they told my parents that if they refused this marriage, they would put me in jail for the rest of my life. So that was the way they forced my parents to accept me being married to one of them. Every evening I was knocked about, punished. I did not know what to do. It was very hard."

Tears well up in her eyes as she tells the story and she stops. The other women come closer and tell her not to be sad, not to cry, that it is over.

"I swear that they really hit me so much, and I really hurt and suffered."

Such simple words to tell such a vile story. This is institutionalised, sanctioned rape and torture. These men saw women that they wanted and they took them because they could, because they had occupied Timbuktu by force and against the will of its inhabitants. They made a mockery of the strict family and religious laws that surround marriage here.

After raping and beating these girls, simply for their pleasure, over the months of the occupation, the extremists did something that is possibly even more evil. When the French arrived and they had to leave, they did so without divorcing the wives they were abandoning. In Islamic law, that means these women cannot marry again. They are denied the joy of ever having a good husband and children of their own. In a culture where marriage and children are everything, are what defines a woman, what gives her place and her meaning, they have been left as outcasts. I can only hope that in the tolerant atmosphere of Timbuktu, a way can be found to release them from this bond so that they can go on to live full lives in their community.

The other girls chimed in with their stories: how they would get told to cover up by the militants - even if they were wearing headscarves or veils, they would be told they weren't heavy enough and would be beaten; how they were told to wear heavier clothes, not their traditional dress, and gloves but they didn't have enough money to buy these things so had to stay in their houses or risk being beaten or put in prison. One girl told me that her father had suffered a heart attack because of the stress and had died. Another asked me to tell people outside Mali what had happened and ask them to send money and help. All of them said that they were frightened that the militants would return, that they were "waiting in the desert."

We see atrocities on our screens every day and it is hard not to become inured to the horrors going on in the world but when you meet people who it has happened to, people just like you and yours, it is different. It is real.

I tried to imagine what it would be like if this had happened in my home town, in Edinburgh. It seems inconceivable. A group of men calling themselves righteous and saying they are coming to give you independence and then taking your daughters because they want to, destroying churches and historical buildings because they can, preventing you from doing any work to earn money to buy food, stopping you from leaving your house because if you do, they will find any excuse to beat you or throw you in prison, forcing you to watch executions in St Andrew's Square …... That is what had happened here, what these people had had to endure.

We were all silent as we left the co-operative. The security guards hurried us into the crew car and we drove off, each absorbed in our own thoughts.

We'd started this quest for a city of gold, a city of myth, the furtherest place on earth. In the time we had spent here, we had seen and heard of the vicissitudes of the occupation but we had also discovered the ending to many of our stories of salt and gold, slaves and learning. Throughout our journey, we had discovered living history, the ties to the past still here in the present. Timbuktu, our goal, was not the glittering capital of Mansa Musa, but it had something that had seduced all of us. Walking down the dusty streets, ever-encroaching into the buildings, past carved wooden doors leading into secret courtyards, we could feel our pace slowing. The warmth of the hospitality to strangers and the openness that met us everywhere we went was overwhelming and humbling.

That hospitality was to reach its crescendo with an invitation to a Touareg party in an area down past the market. There was going to be singing and dancing and Maya had already told me she was going, so I knew I would have at least one friend there. I put on my best kaftan and some lipstick and got ready to party.

When we arrived, young Ahmed and his cousin and brother were waiting, looking extremely smart in their robes and veils. They ushered us in to the courtyard where there was a large tent with rugs scattered on the ground and cushions round the side. Guests were already arriving. We went in to meet our hosts, a musician family. They were famous within the city and played at all the big weddings and celebrations. During the occupation, public music had been banned so not only did they have to play in secret, they also lost their livelihood and had to borrow money and rely on gifts to survive, but those days were gone now and music was back on the streets.

We moved into the tent and they started playing. The father played a form of traditional guitar and sang, his son sang too and his wife languidly played the drums. It sounded a bit like the blues but more upbeat and with an African rhythm. These were master musicians. All the women were sitting at one end of tent and the men were at the other. Dancing was clearly a chance for people to show themselves and their outfits off. The women started.

Two of the women went and sat down in front of the musicians. They were dressed lavishly and had on headdresses made of silver coins with rich veils covering their heads. When they were comfortably seated, they started swaying to the music, moving their heads and arms flirtatiously. A shoulder would twitch, a lip would pout. It was very obviously a courtship dance. These opulent women were insanely sexy without baring or shaking anything. Maya grabbed me and took me into the middle to have a go. I definitely felt like one of the gang as I was handed a veil and shown how to flutter my eyelashes. It was fun and I shimmied with abandon. When my turn was over, one of the women sat me down beside her and braided my hair so she could put a headdress on me. She clicked her tongue with satisfaction at the results. Clearly, my best kaftan and lipstick had not been nearly good enough.

Then it was the men's turn. Young Ahmed started off. He leaped and whirled, twirled and cavorted. There were Cossack moves, cancan kicks and pirouettes that Rudolf Nureyev would have envied. He was like a marvellous dancing frog. I laughed out loud with the sheer hilarity and happiness of it.

The night wore on and the stars came out. The musicians kept playing and the singers sang. Everyone danced and swayed and clapped in a swell of melody. This was what I had come for, this was Timbuktu for me, the joy of the unbreakable human spirit.

THE END

Thanks!

I have a lot of people to thank for helping with the book and with the BBC2 series.

Harry Bell, Owner and Creative Director of Tern TV. Thank you so much for taking such a massive chance on me. You are a brave man! Your belief in the programmes, your energy and your ability to enthuse everyone around you have been an inspiration. Thanks, Harry.

Huge thanks go to the BBC for commissioning the series and seeing it through. Thanks to Tom McDonald and Lucinda Axelsson for their ideas and their support and Rachel Morgan for that initial belief.

The Team at Tern TV have been fantastic all the way through. Thanks to Andrew Blackwell for his genius research; Alicia Arce also known a HOTS – the Holder of The Story –for her brilliant directing and her constant passion and focus; Séamas McCracken for capturing the essence of the things we saw and experienced; Laura Buchan for all the information and her inimical style; "Lucky" Bill Gill for a truly beautiful edit; Angela Smith, Diane Dunbar, and Charlene Myles for the organisation and back up; Paul Wilson for taking the breaths out; and David Strachan for all things book-related.

Thanks to Secret Compass and Ben for keeping us safe.

Epic Morocco (www.epicmorocco.co.uk) organised it all brilliantly on the ground in Morocco but brought so much more to the story than just fixing. Charlie Shepherd knows everyone and everything in the country and got us to all the best bits. He has also been a wonderful friend. It was an absolute pleasure to share this fantastic adventure with you, Charlie. Thanks also to: James Cutting, Simo Hadji, Khalid, Toby, Saaid and Mohamed.

Ismaiel Dicko, was our Fixer in Mali and did an amazing job. I think his phone is actually an extension of his ear. He not only fixed, he was my language tutor as well and his insight and contacts were invaluable. Iniche, Ismaiel.

Thank you to my brother, Robbie Morrison, for reading through the first draft of the book and doing lots of crucial corrections. I owe you a trip to Morocco…

Thank you to my dear friend, Tanya Woolf, for editing the book. I really appreciate it, T.

Thanks to Ken Anderson for the introduction to Tern TV - it is really all down to you!

Thanks to Elsa Trujillo for saving my bacon.

Thank you to Fredi and Jim Morrison, Mum and Dad, for the words of wisdom!

Thank you to the people of Morocco and Mali for sharing their stories.

17933625R00130

Printed in Poland
by Amazon Fulfillment
Poland Sp. z o.o., Wrocław